Betrayal's Baby

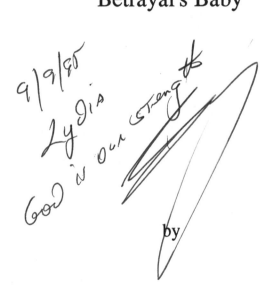

9/9/95
Lydia
God is our strength

by

P. B. Wilson

ISBN 0-9621408-0-5

Dedication

To Mom,

God's
special gift
to me.

Acknowledgements

My sincere thanks to Lela Gilbert, Rhonda Colburn, Marilyn Davis and Jane Berry for their painstaking efforts in editing and critiquing this book.

My appreciation to Dena LeMmons, Mary Proby, Mary Dumas, Dorice Warren and Germaine Benemie for encouraging me through the birthing of this book.

My gratitude to my best friend and husband, Frank, for his tremendous support.

My gratefulness to God for my five daughters who have been God's instruments in continuing to fine-tune my love and perseverance.

To Vida Sparks, the wind beneath my wings.

Table of Contents

Dedication
Acknowledgements

Chapter	Title	Page
One	An Unwanted Child	1
Two	Betrayed	13
Three	Growing Pains	27
Four	I Did It My Way	39
Five	One Step Up	49
Six	A Rude Awakening	59
Seven	The Showdown	67
Eight	My Turn	79
Nine	Putting An Axe to the Root	93
Ten	Getting It Straight	109
Eleven	Eviction Notice	123

Chapter One

AN UNWANTED CHILD

The blanket's warmth and the rhythmic sound of my husband's breathing were unable to lull me to sleep. It was 4 a.m. and I could still visualize a scene that had acted itself out not many days before.

A robust gentleman rose to his feet and politely excused himself as he passed each person sitting in the pew. Making his way to the center aisle, he hurriedly headed for the front of the church auditorium. He was the first to arrive there out of the thousand men and women who would follow. Within seconds, hundreds of others, with tears flooding their faces, streamed into the aisles leading to the altar.

Each of those individuals, at one time or another, had faced betrayal. They hadn't confronted the betrayal that takes place when a citizen commits treason against his country or a trusted employee embezzles company funds. No, the betrayals these people faced were more personal than that. Their cuts went deeper; their pain had been more intense. Their betrayals had taken place when someone they believed in, counted on, or trusted intimately hurt them. For some, the impact had been mental, for others emotional or financial. And in far too many cases, there had been physical abuse.

The suburban middle class New York church where this scene took place is led by a pastor who is academically trained and very knowledgeable in the Word of God. His commitment to his church's membership is highlighted by programs he has instituted to help develop a closer walk with the Lord. And their responsiveness to my message and personal testimony was revealing. On the surface, most of those who came forward appeared to have conquered all of life's common foes, to have scaled Mt. Success and planted the victory flag on top. But underneath the skin, behind the rosy smiles of contentment, were seething and simmering memories of betrayal.

That particular morning, church leaders, teachers, and workers stood among newly committed Christians. They were all admitting that, although they had dealt with many hurts in their lives and had surrendered them to the Lord, a sense of betrayal still haunted them.

Lying there in the darkness, I thought about the countless people who have been critically wounded by others. Having travelled around the world, meeting thousands of people from many cultures, I realized that one common thread runs among them. They, like me, have been betrayed. When that happens, Betrayal has a baby. And that baby's name is Bitterness.

As I lay awake in the shadows of our bedroom, Phillipians 3:10 was once again burning in my soul:

> That I might know Him, the power of His resurrection and the fellowship of His suffering being made conformable to His death.

It seemed as if an invisible hand had pushed the button on an internal tape recorder. Hauntingly the words played over and over. As shadows from the lightly blowing trees outside my window danced around my walls, I meditated on the first five words, "That I might know Him."

Behind closed eyelids, pictures of my first meeting with Frank flashed before me. One of the scenes found us sitting in a health food restaurant. We were both vegetarians. Over large salads, we spent hours solving most of the world's problems. We were opinionated, but respected each other's views. After a couple of weeks of socializing, if someone would have asked, "Do you know Frank Wilson?" my answer would have been, "Yes, I know Frank."

Many years have passed. Times of conversing and observing Frank in different situations have given me insight into how he sees things. During disagreements over a decision reached or a direction taken, I have studied how he arrives at his conclusions. We have shared deep secrets and fears. Times of laughter, disappointments, and tears have been woven into the fiber of our relationship. Each day deepens the intimate fellowship and tremendous love we have for one another. Today, if some were to ask me if I know Frank Wilson, my answer would most assuredly be, "Yes, I *know* Frank".

After years of regular church attendance, a commitment to daily Bible study and devotion time, I felt very strongly that I had come to know Christ. Then I was challenged by the Apostle Paul's own longing and pilgrimage "to *know* Him." Paul wanted "to *know*" Jesus not only on the mountaintops of life but also in the valley of the shadow of death. An honest appraisal of myself revealed that I wanted only the mountaintops and not the valleys. Was it necessary to have both in order to *know* Him?

That night my eyes searched the black, empty ceiling as if an answer lay there. The electric clock on top of the television announced in red numbers that forty-five minutes had passed since my awakening. Turning on my side, the sharp realization that I could be a Christian and not intimately know Christ caused a familiar sense of anxiety. Waves of longing broke across the shores of my soul only to withdraw and return again.

Memories of my atheistic days when I 'ate Christians for lunch' with my rhetorical questions came drifting back. I had been seeking infinite answers to my finite questions. That all had come to a halt, however, the morning I was awakened by the shock of the 1971 California earthquake. Startled out of a sound sleep, I heard glass breaking and electrical lines snapping and felt my bed violently shaking. In the midst of that terrifying experience something even more traumatic happened to me. I, a devout atheist lying in the middle of my bed, sat up and cried, "Oh my God!"

Quickly I thought, "Where did that come from?" My mind had not been clear enough to have thought through that statement. The cry had come from within my depths, from a place untraveled by logic. My inmost soul had called out to the living God! On that day I went from being atheist to agnostic. "Surely," I concluded, "there must be a God". Then in June of 1974 after intense searching and pursuing the question, "Who is this God?" I met His Son, Jesus Christ, and invited Him into my life.

The Door

Now deep in the night, I was back to asking questions again. And this time they were not rhetorical. I was longing for a deeper relationship with Someone who was patiently waiting for me. Jesus states in Revelation 3:20:

> Behold, I stand at the door and knock, if any man hears my voice and opens the door, I will come in and fellowship with him and he with Me.

In this scripture, Jesus was speaking to the Laodicean Church, a group of Christians. Jesus was in their lives, but a locked door prevented His entrance into an abiding fellowship. They knew Him but they didn't *know* Him.

Behind a bolted door were the material possessions in which they had placed their hope and security.

The "knocking" in this verse is not what we are used to, a tapping of three or four times. This is a continuous, 24-hour a day, non-stop knocking. "What kind of God do we serve," I pondered, "who died on the cross for our sins, usually spends years wooing us to a decision to accept Him, then stands at the locked door of our heart and knocks continuously until we open up?" The answer resounded, "A God of Love!"

"*Knowing* Christ is not going to be difficult," I concluded, "because He's waiting and willing for me to know Him." So what then was causing my sleepnessness?

My Locked Door

Locked doors were nothing new to me. Before inviting Christ into my life, acquaintances would often comment on my cold and distant personality. My whole life was a locked door. After all, it's hard for people to hurt you if you don't let them in. I lived in an emotionally constructed castle, with a raised drawbridge and an encircling moat filled with hungry alligators. Upon meeting Frank and believing I would be safe with him, I dropped the drawbridge and allowed him to cross. Once he was inside, I reeled up the bridge and slammed the gate shut. No one else could enter. Later, when I gave my heart to Jesus, that gradually began to change.

I can still hear my pastor saying to the congregation, "According to Romans 10:9, all you have to do to become a Christian and receive eternal life is to acknowledge that you are a sinner, believe that God raised Christ from the dead, and ask Him to come into your heart. You don't have to clean yourself up first. He comes in with a broom, bucket, and mop. Jesus will do the cleaning." He was right. And when Christ entered my life, He had His work cut out for Him. As He made His way through my heart, He knocked before entering each area. It took me a while to realize that His desire was not simply to come in and scrub until it was spotless; equally as important, He wanted to fellowship with me.

Suddenly, my thoughts were disturbed when Frank started talking in his sleep. It sounded as if someone were chasing him in his dream. A few quick shakes and the calling of his name allowed him to drift back into deep slumber. Wishing that a few quick shakes could end my dilemma of wanting to *know* Him, I continued to pursue my train of thought.

I knew that Jesus had been working His way through my heart for over ten years. And I knew that His greatest desire was for fellowhsip. Unfortunately, I had spent most of our time together socializing. Did you know that there is a big difference between socializing and fellowshipping? Socializing is making contact, having light chatter, and eventually, if the conversation goes long enough, giving an opinion. It's entertaining to watch socializing take place. Try sitting in the corner at the next affair you're invited to and observing the people. After greeting each other, they begin to form small clusters. They will bring each other up to date on the latest episodes in their lives. If one cluster stays together for any length of time, they will settle into talking about one topic: sports, children, politics or something similar. As the conversation proceeds, each participating person will begin to give his opinion on the selected topic. Sometimes it can get rather heated, but that's socializing.

Judging from the comments heard in "Christian conversations" and from my participation in counselling sessions, I think it is safe to say that most of us are socializing with Jesus. It's not that we don't hear the call to fellowship. It's just that when we pray and listen to the Lord, He will inevitably address some area of our life in which we need to change. When He does, we decide at that moment either to socialize or fellowship.

Suppose a single Christian man wants to fellowship with Christ. During their time together, the Lord begins addressing the issue of fornication. "My son," Jesus says, "when you have sex outside of marriage, it destroys God's ultimate desire for a man and woman to live holy and sanctified lives. It also grieves the Holy Spirit that lives in you. I am calling you to repent and 'flee fornications'. The young man, who has been thoroughly enjoying his extra-curricular activities, soberly assesses the request. After much thought he responds, "Lord, I just don't believe that You would give me these desires if you didn't expect me to fulfill them." That's his opinion, and fellowship has quickly changed to socializing.

Fellowship with Jesus comes when we align ourslves with His way, Word, and will. Opinions remain only when they agree with the Word of God. Amos 3:3 asks, "Can two walk together unless they be agreed?" As finite creatures, we must be willing to acknowledge that Christ is infinite and all-knowing. We walk by faith, not feeling. For the most part, we understand fellowshipping in theory only until the Lord knocks on one of our locked doors.

Jesus had already made His way through my heart, knocking on doors of fear, revenge, doubt, anxiety, and selfishness (to name a few); I had eventually allowed Him into those areas and had surrendered my opinions in exchange for fellowship. Little did I know that Jesus would one day knock on one particular door that I had hitherto refused to admit was even there.

Camouflaged

I'll never forget the beautiful mansion of a record mogul that Frank and I once visited. The elegant woodwork and the hand-painted wallpaper were breathtaking.

The most intriguing feature of the house, however, was the guest bathroom door off the main entry way. There was no doorknob on the outside. In order to enter, you had to push a certain area of what appeared to be a hand-painted wall, and the door popped open. No one knew the door was there except those who had already been shown the interesting entry.

I had a door like that in my heart. Unnoticeable to the untrained eye, I was able to move through life as if the door didn't exist. That night, it was that hidden door that kept me tossing and turning on my bed. Jesus was knocking.

He was standing at the camouflaged door. How silly of me to think He had just discovered it. All the other doors were connected to this one. He was knocking. It was time.

I jerked the electric blanket aside and hurried to the one place in my house where, generally, I am not interrupted: the bathroom. Kneeling beside the tub, I pictured myself running to open the hidden door. As the door was thrown open, Jesus smiled and entered. There was a special chair prepared for Him.

Taking a seat at His feet and with tears streaming down my face, I sat in humble silence. Finally I whispered, "Lord, I love You. I've been awake thinking about knowing You. The Apostle Paul said that he wanted to 'know You and the power of Your resurrection'. I do, too."

Jesus caressed my face and replied, "Paul also said that he wanted to know Me in the 'fellowship of My suffering'. You cannot have one without the other." He then questioned, "Are you prepared?"

Doubt gripped my heart for a moment but my commitment to know Him moved me forward. Answering His question with a question, I responded. "How can I suffer with you, Lord? Your Word says that the 'Foxes have holes and the birds have nests, but the Son of Man had nowhere to lay His head.' I can't suffer that way. I have a place to stay." I continued, "Your Word also says that You were beaten beyond recognition and crucified on the cross. You suffered crucifixion on the cross for our sins. I am sinful and surely wouldn't be called to die for someone else's sins." With pleading in my heart, I stated, "If You tell me how I can suffer for You, I will do it."

Jesus looked deep into my eyes and said, "When I walked the face of the earth, I had twelve close friends. One of them sold Me for thirty pieces of silver. The others ran and hid in fear. I was betrayed. But I forgave them and loved them."

By now I knew where He was taking the conversation. We had been there before but, in the past, I had swiftly changed our fellowship to socializing. Hesitantly I inquired, "What do You want me to do?" He responded, "I want you to forgive your mother and love her."

From somewhere within the room a whining sound began to rise. The sound was familiar. It had never been that loud before, but I recognized it immediately.

Betrayal's Baby

I covered my ears hoping to stop the sound but it came from within. It was Betrayal's baby. Its name is Bitterness.

In my imagination, I see a green slimy creature covered with infectious boils. It has a foul odor and whines all the time. Bitterness comes into the world holding a clock in its hand that is set to the exact day, hour and minute of betrayal. That clock is placed over the fireplace of our hearts. With each new betrayal, an additional clock joins the collection. With every clock comes a "commitment of protection" that we hope will keep us from experiencing the same kind of pain and disappointment again.

Some women say, "I'll never love a man the way I loved
him." Other men and women proclaim, "I'll never trust
anyone again." Still others have announced, "I'm looking
out for number one!" The clock reminds us that, at some
point or other, we chose to trust someone only to be
misused. We've committed ourselves to self-protection,
and those commitments have frozen and imprisoned our
emotions with regard to every future relationship.

I had always known Bitterness was in my heart. But I
had locked it in a forgotten closet. Out of sight, out of
mind might have worked except for one problem: Bitterness whines constantly. No wonder I had difficulty sleeping ... Jesus kept knocking continuously on the door of my
heart and Bitterness never ceased to whine.

As I sat looking into the face of Jesus, Bitterness pulled
my mother's clock off the fireplace and began to shake it
in my face. It chided, "You can never forgive her for the
things she has done to you. Even if you tried to forgive
her, you can never forget. With each memory comes pain.
So why even try?" Bitterness threw its head back in
laughter.

Nodding in agreement, I knew Bitterness was right. I
had tried to forgive her in the past but failed; each new
hurt seemed greater than the one before. Tonight,
however, was different. In the past, I'd wanted to forgive
her so I could be free of the pain. This aching now felt in
my heart, however, was caused by my desire to fellowship
with Christ. The realization that I could never know Him
if I weren't willing to "fellowship in His sufferings" became a reality.

Jesus sat quietly. There was compassion in His eyes,
but otherwise He sat motionless. This was my decision.
"I have a right to be bitter," I thought. Bitterness, seeing
my hesitation, danced around the room, assuming victory.
I drew back, understanding that forgiveness required me
to give up my right to judge my mother's motivations.

"That would mean she goes free," I considered. Somewhere within my self, I wanted her to pay.

I thought about what I would be giving up if I decided to hold onto my right to bitterness. Jesus would smile and tell me how much He loved me. He would then get up from the chair, leave the room, and close the door. Shortly thereafter the knocking would begin again until I chose to allow Him to enter. The process would start all over again.

As I looked at the Lord, a burning rose within—a burning to know Him. Never again did I want to force Him to stand at a door of my heart and knock, seeking fellowship with me. He's already given His life. A quiet determined voice stated, "Lord, I want You more than my right to be bitter. What do You want me to do?"

Without hesitation He replied, "I want you to call your mother and set up a meeting. Go to listen. I will tell you what to say."

The unwanted child in my life, Bitterness, looked worried. I felt a sense of satisfaction. The next morning, I called Mom.

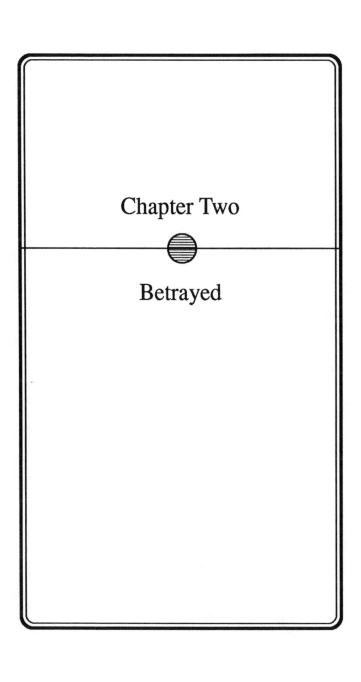

Chapter Two

Betrayed

Chapter Two

BETRAYED

It was easy to remember men and women who have been betrayed. I could never forget their faces as they recounted to me those painful parts of their lives. All of the stories in this chapter are true; however, the names have been changed. Perhaps you will catch a glimpse of your own life as you read.

Wounded

Rushing past the ticket agent and onto the plane, I heard the stewardess closing the door behind me. There was only one seat left. Briefly glancing at the woman who sat on the aisle and at the elderly man sitting next to the window, I tossed my belongings in the upper bin. I made my way to the middle seat giggling inwardly as I noticed the gentleman's hat. It was like a baseball cap but there was a clock on the front that actually worked. The words 'No Time To Lose' were printed above it. "Dennis is my name, what's yours?" he inquired. The twinkle in his eyes and the lilt in his voice told me I was in for an interesting flight.

We had barely left the ground and it seemed like I had known Dennis all my life. He was fascinating. At seventy-three years of age, he had survived four surgeries and was presently recovering from a stroke. And now he was on his way to Los Angeles to spend time with his girlfriend!

Dennis' children had been adults before he decided to complete his high school education. He'd earned a degree in engineering, made wise investments with his money, and had become very wealthy. He owned prize dogs and horses. His hilltop house in Oakland was built around a redwood tree.

With a broad smile, he proudly informed me, "I have one daughter. She's my pride and joy. She'll be at the airport to pick me up when I arrive." He turned his head momentarily towards the window.

"Do you have any other children?" I asked.

Dennis looked as if he wished I hadn't asked that question. His voice dropped to a whisper as he replied, "I also have a son, but I haven't talked to him for over a year. You see, the doctors didn't think I was going to make it through my last heart operation. I called him to my bedside and gave him instructions and power of attorney."

Dennis paused and looked out the window. I could see that he was struggling with painful memories. He continued, "After my recovery, I discovered that my son had gone into my bank account and withdrawn $100,000. I just don't understand it! He could have had anything I owned if he'd only asked. Instead he stole from me. We haven't talked since." His eyes dimmed with sadness.

Dennis was betrayed and Betrayal had a baby.

Deserted

My husband, Frank, and I were speaking at a conference when a petite, middle-aged woman approached me. "Hello, my name is Lucy. I know you're really busy, but I was wondering if we could talk this weekend. You said something in your message that affected me deeply." I searched Lucy's face and saw the deep pain I had encountered in many different cities and on many different occasions. Whenever I share my own story with groups of people, there are always those who relate to my hurts. They somehow know that I will understand their innermost wounds.

I agreed to talk with Lucy the next morning. As I walked to meet her, I couldn't help wondering what form betrayal had taken in her life. I found her in the lobby of the hotel. Lucy had selected a sofa in the fartherst corner of the room. When I sat down, I noticed she was trembling. Taking her hand, I began to pray that God would direct our time together. She calmed down a little and waited a moment before speaking. "I am forty-two years old and have lived a nightmare most of my life." It was as if she had rehearsed that statement all night. After getting the words out, she released a deep sigh.

"I didn't think anyone would understand," she continued. "I hate my mother and it has affected my whole life! My marriage was a disaster, and now I am completely miserable."

"Lucy, why don't you start at the beginning?" I asked.

"I have six brothers and sisters," she said. "When I was nine years old, my father died and my mother was left to raise us. It was very difficult, but there was a sense of security in the fact that we were family. Then two years later, I saw Mother packing her suitcase. My heart sank. When I asked her where she was going, she said she was going away for about six weeks and that we kids would be staying with various relatives. My older brother and I went to one aunt's home."

Lucy stopped and shook her head sadly before she went on. "Shortly after we got there, my brother began to make sexual advances towards me. I didn't understand what he was doing, and I didn't know who I could talk to. 'It's o.k.,' I thought. 'Mommy will be back soon and she'll know what to do.' But the six weeks passed and we didn't hear from her. At about that time, my brother molested me, and as it turned out, my mother didn't come back for six years!"

By now tears were pouring down Lucy's face. She wrung her hands in her lap. I quietly asked, "For how long did your brother molest you?"

Through sobs she answered, "The whole time my mother was gone. I was so ashamed, so afraid and guilty. I'll never forget the day my mother came back to get us. She acted like she had never left. She had gifts for everyone and never explained where she had been or what she had been doing. I hated her for leaving me so alone and vulnerable!"

In telling her story, Lucy removed her finger from the crack in the emotional dam which had held her sorrow for over thirty years. It seemed as if pain and misery were flowing from every pore in her body. I moved close and held her in my arms. I don't know how many minutes passed, but finally Lucy sat up and composed herself until she was able to go on.

"I left my mother's home when I was eighteen years old and moved to another city. I got a job and after a few years met and married a man that I felt would be a good husband. He was really special. We got along well, but our sex life was terrible. He complained because I was always so distant. He was right! I wanted to reach out and touch him, to love him, but I just couldn't. My marriage ended in a childless divorce. So here I am—forty-two years old, lonely, angry and miserable. I want to be free of these feelings. I really do, but I'm caught in a web, and the harder I struggle to get free, the worse it gets."

"Lucy," I asked, "Did your husband know about what your brother did to you?"

"No," she responded.

"Did you ever tell your mother what happened?" I questioned. Once again she responded, "No."

Lucy had been carrying her hurt and shame alone for thirty years! I wondered if the coldest, darkest rat-infested dungeon in the world could equal the emotional prison she'd lived in.

Lucy was betrayed and Betrayal had a baby.

Rejected

Physical betrayal is just one of the many forms betrayal takes. The story of Sam and Dorothy typifies another.

Sam was in love with the woman of his dreams. Dorothy was the most sensitive, charming and alluring woman he had ever met. For once he didn't allow his natural shyness to hinder him. He boldly proposed marriage, and soon he was whisking her away to live happily ever after. Surely their marriage had been made in heaven!

Two years later, the happy couple began having children. Getting up in the middle of the night and changing diapers was a pleasure for Sam. He was more than willing to share the task of raising a family. And when his eldest son grew to an age when Sam believed he should know right from wrong, the young father began to take disciplinary action.

"I'll never forget the first time I spanked Edward," Sam told me. "Dorothy began to scream and told me never to do that again! I ignored her. Knowing he was our firstborn, I thought she was just over-reacting."

Dorothy bore three more children, and Sam and Dorothy's love remained strong and healthy. Their only major problem arose when Sam took steps to discipline their children. "I never spanked them in anger," Sam explained. "I know the Bible teaches that a father should not provoke his children to anger. I also know that if you spare the rod, you will spoil the child. Yet I could never get Dorothy to see it. The 'straw that broke the camel's back' was one day when I spanked our daughter, Priscilla."

"What happened, Sam?" I asked.

"Well, Priscilla continued to be disobedient in a particular area. After having a long talk with her, I gave her a spanking. Suddenly, out of nowhere, Dorothy appeared. She jumped on my back and began to scratch and claw at my face! She was like a wild animal! I became so angry that I hit her. I had never struck a woman before, much less the woman I loved."

Sam hadn't chosen to seek professional help. At the time, he had been young and, in retrospect, he felt he had been too selfish to realize that the problem with Dorothy had very little to do with him and almost everything to do with her past. Sam felt he couldn't stand by and watch his marriage deteriorate. But he also knew that if he spanked the children, he would have to physically fight Dorothy. Although he seldom spanked them, he knew it was something he would have to do if necessary.

"One of the hardest things I have ever done was to pack my bags and leave the woman and children I love," Sam told me sadly. "I thought I was doing the noble thing."

When I inquired about Dorothy's past, Sam explained that Dorothy's mother had died when she was a child. She had deeply loved her mother. A few years after her death, Dorothy's father had remarried. Her stepmother had been selfish, as well as verbally and physically abusive. She often beat Dorothy and locked her in her room. Dorothy felt betrayed by her father who turned a deaf ear to her pleas for help, and when Dorothy's father died, her stepmother threw her out of the house.

Afte a long court battle, Dorothy had been awarded legal title to her father's house. It was a house full of haunting memories of a deceased mother, a cruel step-mother, and a father who wouldn't listen. She had carried those memories into her marriage with Sam, and those memories had destroyed still another family. Dorothy was not a villain but a victim. As a result, Sam and her children had become victims, too.

Dorothy was betrayed and Betrayal had a baby.

Deceived

Douglas had worked hard to open his own business. He loved the Lord and had been diligent in acquiring the knowledge he would need to make wise financial investments for himself and his clients.

"I wanted to be able to give my clients solid and honest advice about investing their money," said Douglas. "I also dreamed of helping some up and coming men and women in the business. I hadn't had anyone to offer me a helping hand. There had been many nights when I lay awake in my bed wondering what I should do next. This business is so competitive that no one wanted to exchange information. So now I wanted to share my knowledge with others."

Meeting Jeff Lawton seemed an answer to his prayer. He was intelligent and motivated and professed to know Christ as his Savior. "When I brought Jeff into the company I thought, 'Now this is a man I would like to invest time in.' It wasn't unusual for us to stay up past midnight reviewing a client's portfolio. Jeff had a lot of school knowledge but needed help with his business sense. Little by little, I began turning my clients over to him when I felt he was qualified."

Douglas continued, "After a few years when the business was really taking off, Jeff announced that he would be leaving. Although I thought it was premature, I was willing to support him in his decision. What he didn't tell me was that he was moving his offices across the hall and taking some of my clients with him! I'll never forget the day he hung his business sign outside his office. I couldn't say now if I was angry, disgusted or depressed. I numbly sat at my desk with tears running down my face. That day my heart was broken and my trust in people shattered."

Douglas was betrayed and Betrayal had a baby.

Unprotected

Patricia was raised by her grandmother. When she was two years old, her nineteen-year-old mother didn't want the responsibility of raising Patricia. After all, the world was waiting for her—a child would weigh her down.

Patricia's father, who planned to make his first million by the time he reached age thirty, took Patricia to his mother's house and asked if she would look after her for a little while. The girl was a teenager before that "little while" ended. Although she loved her grandmother, she ached over the absence of her father and mother.

As a child, Patricia never had a birthday party. She saw her cousins going to parties wearing pretty dresses and knew she would wear those same dresses once they were passed down to her. Later, as a teenager, she blossomed into a strikingly beautiful, straight-A student. Patricia felt her hard work in school would earn her the praise and admiration of her father. Her father did notice her and asked that she move in with him. Her dream had come true.

Thrilled at the attention he had begun to shower upon her, Patricia worked even harder. She relished every word of encouragement and approval. Voted the most popular girl in school, Patricia was also editor of the school newspaper, cheerleader and president of the debating team.

She was sitting on top of the world. Then one day, her father decided to introduce her to the facts of life. Sadly, it was not to be through conversation. This beautiful, intelligent young girl was now an incest victim. It took her weeks to get up the courage to tell her grandmother—weeks of agonizing guilt and shame.

"Why would he do this to me? What did I do to make him treat me this way? Was it my fault?" Questions echoed in her mind. Finally she confided in her closest friend, her grandmother.

As she poured out the tragic details, her grandmother slowly shook her head from side to side. When Patricia finished, she reached over, patted her hand, and said, "You may be my granddaughter, but I know my son. He would never do anything like that. Why don't you tell me the truth. Have you gotten into trouble with one of the boys in school?"

The pain of her grandmother's denial was every bit as intense as the agony she still suffered at the hands of her father. As she returned to her father's house, she started wondering if she had somehow imagined the whole thing. Eventually, a family friend arrived at home one day while she was being molested. Once this friend reported it to the grandmother, the truth was out.

Help came but not soon enough. In her despair and confusion, Patricia plunged into a life of promiscuity. She felt worthless. Finally she reached a point where she didn't want to go on living. Only the love of a caring spouse rescued her.

Patricia was betrayed and Betrayal had a baby.

Deadly

The high school senior picture of a gorgeous blond flashed across the television screen. The news anchorman listed her accomplishments, including pictures of her wedding. The bridegroom was an attractive young man.

This woman, whose name was Stacy, had worked to put her husband through four years of college followed by medical school. Even after her three children were born, she continued to work two jobs. Stacy longed for the day when all the student loans would be paid off, and at long last, that day arrived. Stacy's husband, Greg, became a successful and prosperous doctor. They moved into a high-class suburban community and joined the country club. Stacy's dreams of happiness were fulfilled. Then devastating news changed her delight into despair. Stacy discovered that her husband was having an affair with his attractive young receptionist.

Stacy confronted her husband about the relationship, but he stubbornly refused to stop seeing Elaine. He filed for divorce and when it was final, he and Elaine were married. Early one foggy morning about a year after the wedding, Stacy got into her car and drove to Greg and Elaine's home. She used a doorkey she had stolen from one of her children. She found her way to the bedroom and shot Greg and Elaine to death as they lay sleeping in their bed.

Today Stacy is in prison and nothing has been accomplished—except that her heartbreak supposedly has been vindicated.

Stacy was betrayed and Betrayal had a baby. Sometimes bitterness, left to its own devices, can be lethal. That is a sobering thought.

An Escape

Many are the stories of betrayal. You probably have one or two of your own which may seem smaller or larger than the ones you've just read. Our lives seem to be filled with numerous tiny betrayals as well as enormous ones.

I have spent a great deal of time with some very committed Christians. Most of them have worked diligently to reconcile poor relationships and to forgive people who have hurt them. Still I never cease to be amazed at how many of us have one deep ultimate betrayal—one so painful that we would rather fold it up and tuck it away in a forgotten closet than ever think about it again. We may say, "It happened a long time ago," or, "It won't do any good to think about it," or perhaps, "Nothing will change." None of these excuses should keep us from facing the facts.

I hope as you read through this book you will do what I did. I hope you'll go to the forgotten closet, unfold the betrayal, and take a long hard look at it. Then through the power of God's Word and His precious Holy Spirit, I pray that you'll get free. I must warn you, however, that this will not be a painless process.

I have reserved the following page for your story of betrayal. Let it remain blank until you feel whole enough to write it in. You will find my story written throughout the pages of this book. I am free to write mine because the pain is gone. Just as Jesus rose from the dead, completely healed, with the nail marks in His hands and feet, so my scars remain. They aren't there to remind me of the pain, but as a testimony to God's healing power. A songwriter wrote, "He'll turn your scars into stars, your wounds into weapons, and your mountains into goldmines."

Don't go on reading without asking Jesus to join you. You're going to need Him right there with you as you finally face up to your own story — a story of your Betrayal and of Betrayal's baby.

Your Story

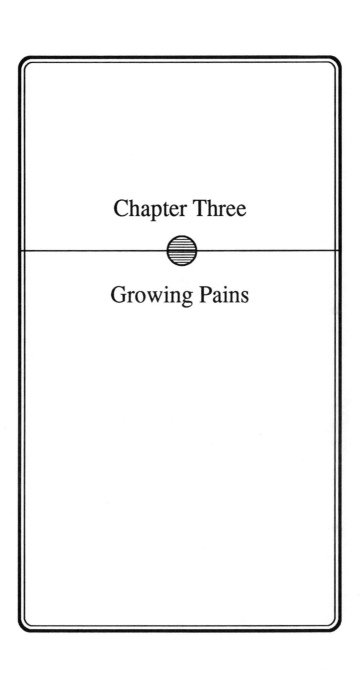

Chapter Three

Growing Pains

Chapter Three

GROWING PAINS

Frantically moving from house to house, the beautiful brunette knocked at every door, inquiring in broken English, "Have you seen my little daughter? She's two years old. I turned my back for a minute and she was gone!" One by one, people who had no information regarding the lost child shook their heads. Fear gripped the woman's heart as pictures of her daughter's possible harm flickered through her mind. A noon train howled, passing only a short distance from the back of her apartment building. She shuddered, imagining her little girl climbing onto the tracks.

Making a mad dash back to her flat, she felt as if she were moving in slow motion. With every step, anxiety snapped at her heels. She decided to search the apartment one last time as she waited for the police to arrive. Tearing through closets and looking behind every large article of furniture, she finally fell on her knees beside the overstuffed sofa in the children's playroom. The old fashioned couch sat on raised legs. A second sense caused her to look underneath. Her two year old, oblivious to all the attention she was getting, was curled up and tucked inside her favorite blanket, taking her afternoon nap.

The mother thought, "How could one little girl cause so much trouble?" Little did she know. It was just the beginning! That day she had found me. Two years prior, she had saved me. It would be thirty-five years before I would be able to thank her from a sincerely grateful heart.

Three Is A Crowd

It was a distraught father who brought home the small white pill from the hospital where he worked as an orderly assistant. There seemed to be no other solution. Although it was like yesterday, two years had passed since the birth of his son. Four months ago he had stood at the bedside of his wife as their first daughter was born. Tears had filled his eyes as he quietly asked, "What's wrong with her?"

Exhausted and in a state of semi-consciousness, his wife murmured helplessly, "The doctors say she is retarded. She has water on the brain."

As she drifted back to sleep, he took the fragile and deformed baby in his arms. His heart filled with love. He whispered to his motionless wife, "Her name will be Elizabeth, like yours."

Now, driving home four months later, there was no doubt in his mind what must happen. News that my mother was pregnant again had all but sent him over the edge. His low income, their sleepless nights with "Little Lizzie", and the tremendous pressure of keeping up with a rambunctious two-year-old son was more, he thought, than either he or his wife could bear.

Unwilling to listen to reason, he insisted that she take the pill that would supposedly abort the child. Slowly, her trembling hands put the pill in her mouth. When my father turned his head, she spit it out and pretended to swallow it as she drank the water. She saved my life.

Life Goes On

Three years after I was born, my dear sister Elenor was born. By age six, I had almost figured the world out. A father has three jobs. He comes home every day at 4 p.m., has dinner with the family, and tells jokes. My older brother taught me and Elenor that we were never to laugh at his jokes. Supposedly that demonstrated mental toughness and was intended to get under my father's skin. I always laughed anyway. Right after dinner, a father leaves for another job and you see him the next day at 4 p.m.

A mother stays home with the children and keeps the house and the children spotless, even if that means they change clothes three times a day.

Also, a mother never sleeps. She's awake when you get up in the morning and she's awake when you go to bed at night.

There was, however, one puzzle with one missing piece. I wondered, "If a mother has four children and they all belong to her, why does she treat them so differently?"

Little Lizzie received understandable attention. One of us had to be with her at all times because we never knew when she would have a seizure. Many nights, she was rushed to the hospital to repair a deep gash somewhere on her body resulting from a fall. Providing comic relief to Lizzie's tragic plight, everything my older brother, Cliff, did was cute. And Elenor, whom we called "Bootsie," was the delightful baby in the family.

Meanwhile, all of my attempts to get equal time were unsuccessful. There was a large love hole in my heart that grew bigger every day. Aggressive and outspoken, my schemes to gain attention had continued to fail miserably. I needed love and approval from my mother, but she constantly pushed me away. She wasn't there for me. It didn't matter to me that she was from Germany and was struggling to learn English. Nor did it concern me that she was forever racing behind my older brother, tending to mentally retarded Lizzie, and diapering baby sister Elenor. I felt betrayed and Betrayal had a baby. Bitterness set up residency in my heart. I turned all my affections toward my father. What a painful experience that must have been for the woman who had saved my life against his "better judgment".

Conclusions

My growing older gave Bitterness the opportunity to develop. This unwanted child moved freely through my thoughts and emotions. Soon Bitterness invited its friends, Rebellion and Anger, to join in on the daily activities. They had a great time orchestrating my response to various events and circumstances.

The clock of commitment is held in the hand of Bitterness at the time of its birth. The clock does not tick and its hands are frozen to the time of the betrayal. Bitterness placed that clock over the fireplace of my heart. It knew that every decision I made in life would be affected by my commitments of protection. I was learning to protect myself from ever being put in a position to be hurt the same way again. By the time I was twelve years old, I had drawn a couple of conclusions about life and made some commitments of protection:

> • *No one but my father cares about me. Therefore, he is the only one worthy of my attention and affections. I'll never let anyone else get close enough to hurt me.*

- *From the looks of things, marriage is like prison. Dad works constantly and Mom's life leaves a lot to be desired. The routine of raising children and cleaning house day after day isn't for me! I'm never getting married or having children.*

- *With Dad gone most of the time, the majority of the orders and directions come from my mother and I lost respect for her long ago! I vowed, "When I grow up, no one is going to tell me what to do!"*

Manifestations

Bitterness skillfully twisted and distorted my personality and outlook on life. The natural gifts given to me by God were covered in a dark shroud, totally disguising my true appearance. My talent for telling creative stories passed through the screen of Bitterness and surfaced as lying. I was an expert. I would lie for the fun of it and no one knew the difference.

My natural wit evolved into sarcasm. My gift to teach became condescending and critical when I gave instructions or even helpful hints. My gift to speak was twisted with a stammering tongue. This speech impediment was so great that I had to think three sentences ahead of myself, changing the words I knew I couldn't pronounce before reaching them. Few people knew the extent of this emotional blockage. The distortions in my personality caused by Bitterness affected my every relationship and decision.

At thirteen, Bitterness had set the stage. The players were in place and a great deal of time had gone into the production. I read the script perfectly.

It was a late summer afternoon. The sweltering heat had risen to the second floor of our home and hung like a wet blanket. Mom passed me at the top of the stairs, making a right towards her room. When she asked me to complete a household task she had assigned earlier in the day, I sharply responded with, "I *did* finish it!" and stormed into my bedroom.

Thinking she was headed in another direction, I was surprised to see her turn the corner into my room. I was standing in the middle of the floor with a smirk on my face. The burning sting of a slap across my face sent Bitterness racing to the fireplace of my heart. Collecting the original clock of betrayal and those that had joined it in the ensuing years of my life, Bitterness held them close to its chest while chanting in my ear, "She hates you! You can see it in her eyes. Are you just going to stand there and take this?"

Within seconds, painful years of rejection erupted in the core of my being. Having little knowledge of the sacrifices paid by my mother to birth and raise me, I was looking coldly into the face of what seemed to be the enemy. Rebellion and Anger joined Bitterness in its taunting. Mom stood squarely in front of me, her gray eyes glinting with indignation, almost daring me to strike back. Anger clouded my vision as my right hand swiftly connected with the side of my mother's face. I shouted, "I hate you and I wish you weren't my mother!"

As if from nowhere, my father appeared and pulled us apart, because by now we had a fighting grip on each other's clothing. He mumbled a few words and removed my mother from the room. Falling across the bed in tearless anger, I felt no remorse. I had done absolutely nothing to deserve such unfair treatment! Bitterness reached into its bag and placed another clock on the mantlepiece of my heart. "No one will ever again lay hands on me!" Such was another commitment of protection.

A short time later, my father came in to console me. He was my knight in shining armor, and he always came to my rescue.

Going Downhill

There would be no more physical altercations with Mom. However, our intense verbal abuse was just as damaging, affecting us both deeply.

My mother had been raised in an environment where a kind word was seldom spoken, a soft touch never felt. Her childhood experiences had left her scarred. Words of encouragement and compliments were not part of her vocabulary. Her way of "helping me get better" seemed to be by telling me everything that was wrong about me. Her pessimistic outlook on life and my negative attitude complimented each other.

I became furious whenever someone would say, "You're just like your mother." Yet, it was true. Both of us were angry and bitter, and we ignited each other like kerosene and fire. Her frustrations with me were reflected in her caustic statements which many times, were unprovoked.

As we watched a soap opera one afternoon, a young woman with an antagonistic attitude appeared on the screen. My mother muttered, "She's evil just like you!" Then she repeated some other all-too-familiar observations: "You will never have friends. People don't like you as soon as they meet you."

When I was a young girl, I vividly remember seeing Mom holding a one-year-old child. As I extended my arms to hold the little girl, she began to cry. My mother announced, "See? Even this child knows you're evil. She can sense it!" Naturally, I believed her.

One Saturday spring afternoon, Bootsie, Lizzie, and I were home alone with Mom. My sixteenth birthday had passed a few months earlier. Something set off an argument between me and my mother. As tempers flared and the words became more heated, my anger reached a boiling point. My mother commanded me to go to my room. Stomping halfway up the stairs, I turned to look out the front door, which was short distance from the bottom step. The wooden door was wide open and the only thing keeping me from freedom was the thin screen door. It had been designed to keep out insects, not keep in a rebellious child.

Bitterness rose to its feet shouting, "Go!" My hand slammed against the screen door latch. I stormed across the porch and headed down the walkway.

My mother raced after me and screamed, "Bunny! Come back here!"

I spun around on my heel. As neighbors on their front porches watched, I yelled, "I hate you, witch!" I took off, glancing back just in time to catch the expression on my mother's face. Her look of dejection is forever etched in my memory. "It serves her right!" said an inner voice, which I thought was my own. Bitterness sat smiling in a comfortable chair in the livingroom in my heart after it had whispered that vicious thought in my mind.

After walking miles, I returned home, went straight to my room, and shut the door. Hours later, I awoke to find my father sitting on the edge of my bed. "Bunny," he said, "I understand you had a problem with Mom today." Without turning to face him, I said, "She hates me. The other day she said she never wanted me."

My father shrugged, "Well, you know how your mother is."

"I want to go to a foster home!" I declared.

"No, I don't think that will work. Just be patient and I will talk to Mom," Dad responded.

There was no chastisement about my encounter with my mother. I don't know what Dad said to Mom, but I had heard him say in the past when they had a disagreement about me, "Why don't you get off the girl's back!" There was no doubt that Dad had chosen to focus on the positives in my character and Mom on the negative. In retrospect, however, his over-compensation to encourage me (even when I was wrong) strengthened my resolve against my mother.

When I finally saw Mom, she tried to get me to understand that I had misunderstood her when she said she never wanted me. There was no interest on my part to listen to her explanation. She was the enemy.

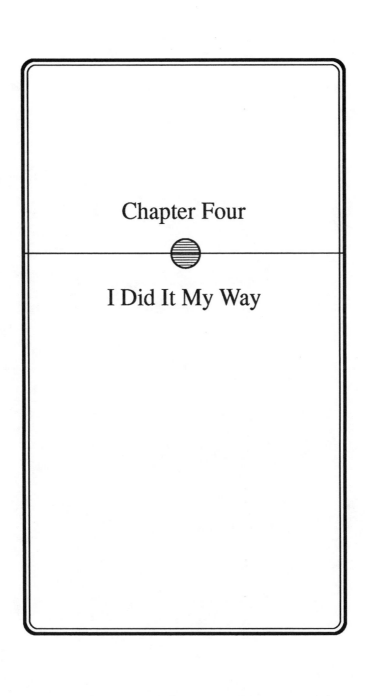

Chapter Four

I Did It My Way

Chapter Four

I DID IT MY WAY

Sighing deeply, I tried to focus my attention on my mother's conversation. "The most terrible thing about World War II was the sirens. We heard them before the bombs started dropping over Germany," she remembered. "Many times it would be at night. We weren't allowed to turn on any lights. All of us in the orphanage would have to quickly line up, go down the spiral staircase, and find our shoes and coats in the dark. Then we would head for the bomb shelter. As a young girl, I was very frightened."

Although I'd heard the story at least a hundred times, I wanted to appear to be interested. So I asked, "If you had a mother, why were you put in an orphanage?"

Mom replied, "Don't forget that I was born in 1927 out of wedlock. In those days, it was a disgrace. There were no daycare centers and people weren't kind to what they called a 'bastard child.' Your grandmother put me in the orphanage because she had to go to Switzerland to get work. Although I was in the orphanage, she paid for my lodging and clothing."

"What was it like in the orphanage?" I half-heartedly asked. Mom responded, "It was terrible. The building was huge and encircled by a high wall. The Catholic nuns were mean and didn't smile. I don't think I ever heard an encouraging word. We got up very early and worked hard in between our school classes. I was very lonely."

Feeling comfortable excusing myself from the table after asking the second question, I rose quickly. Mom said, "Bunny, you don't know how lucky you are to have a home and a mother and father raising you. I don't even know my father's name."

Forcing a smile, I answered, "I know, Mom." I hesitated for barely a second before I asked, "Can I go down to Jeannie's house now?"

Mom sadly nodded her head. Once again, she had been unable to breach my impregnable wall. I didn't care that she had a difficult childhood! Her lack of love, acceptance, and approval towards me had made me bitter. How could I have known that I was demanding of her something that she didn't have to give? Those gifts had never been given to her.

Free At Last

An imaginary calendar hung on my bedroom wall with lines drawn through each passing day. High school graduation would be my passport away from home. Soon after receiving my diploma, my luggage was placed in the trunk of our car and I was driven 200 miles to enroll in secretarial school. It would take one year to complete the course.

My excitement over leaving home would have been dampened had I realized that extra baggage had been put in the car. As I turned in my seat to wave goodbye out the back window to my brother and sister, Bitterness turned and waved also. It had packed its bag too and was going with me.

Ohio Career College in Columbus, Ohio, marked the beginning of a "free" life. It wasn't, however, my choice. I had no desire to be a secretary. My father had felt that since I hadn't chosen a career and didn't want to go to college, a vocation was essential. Grudgingly, I agreed upon secretarial school. A year didn't seem too long a time to invest in a short-term career.

The four hour drive with Dad passed quickly. It gave him the opportunity to review everything he had attempted to teach me while growing up. At one point he chuckled to himself, "What are you laughing about?" I inquired.

He answered, "Do you remember when you were eight years old and your aunt in Washington wanted you to come visit? I took you to the train station and while we were standing on the platform waiting for the conductor to call for boarding, I started feeling anxious about my little girl going such a long distance. Looking down on your head of brown curls, I said, 'I sure hate to see you go on such a long trip.' I thought you might begin to cry and say you didn't want to go. Instead you looked up at me very nonchalantly and announced, 'Well Dad, a girl has to leave home sometimes!"

Throwing his head back in an uproarious laugh, Dad winked and said, "I knew right then that you were going to be all right. You're just like your Dad."

Being "just like" my father meant I was independent and aggressive. Beginning as an orderly in a hospital, Dad had numerous jobs before becoming an insurance agent. Awards lined his basement office. His success had afforded us trips around the country. He had pulled himself up by his own bootstraps. It was only natural that I would follow in his footsteps.

A New Home

The dormitory, two blocks from the college, was an old high-rise apartment building built sixty years before I first stepped into its lobby. Each floor had three apartments, each housing four girls. Determining within a few days that the apartment next to mine was nicer and that the girls in it were more fun, I put my talent for lying to good use.

I manipulated my way into the other apartment in spite of the strict rules that no one could change rooms.

That year is a long blur of daydreaming through classes I didn't want to attend. My commitment of protection to never allow anyone to tell me what to do surfaced with all my teachers and dormitory counselors. I was the student with a "chip on her shoulder." And their opinions of me didn't matter.

However, away from the constant reminder that I "couldn't make friends," my God-given personality began to take root and grow. Although my natural wit would often come out sarcastically, it made people laugh. No one knew the depth of my pain because the negative experiences with my mother were not shared with anyone. The relationships I developed were fun but superficial. Bitterness had frozen my feelings, and the clocks on my fireplace did not tick. They remained set to the minute, hour, and day of my betrayals. It was important that no one get close enough to either pick up one of my clocks or add another to the fireplace.

California Or Bust

Graduation came quickly. Then came the decision of what to do next. The clocks sitting on my fireplace reminded me that returning to Youngstown to live in the same house with my mother was not an option. A telephone conversation with my father gave me the direction needed. "Bunny," Dad said in an unusually serious tone, "you know I've spent time in Los Angeles. The business opportunities there are great. My recommendation, honey, is that you go and stay with your cousin Angie until you can find a job and get your own place."

My deliberation time was short. Dad was always right. So, soon after finishing secretarial school, the plane carrying me, my dreams, and Bitterness touched down at Los

Angeles International Airport. I was thrilled to be in a place where the sun always shone. The palm trees seemed to call my name when the sliding glass doors opened at the baggage claim. Within a surprisingly short period of time, I had acquired a job, an apartment, and a car.

For all practical purposes, I was content. Going and coming as I pleased and answering to no one at home was utopia. My only struggles were job related. Unfortunately, unless you own the company, there is always going to be someone in authority who has the right to tell you what to do. My commitment to protection wouldn't allow that.

After being fired from three consecutive jobs for outspoken and belligerent behavior, I began to reassess my communication skills. There had to be a way to mask my animosity towards authority. Learning the principles of tact helped keep me at my next position longer. When I disguised my disdain for supervision, my career took a positive turn. I was refining the fine art of being a trained manipulator, liar and deceiver.

Surprise!

Eight years had passed since I had drawn my first conclusions about life and made my original commitments of protection. My earlier assessments of life remained unchanged. But now new ones were added:

> • *People are essentially weak and need to believe in God as a crutch. The only time God becomes important to them is when they are in trouble. I am not weak and do not need a crutch; therefore, there is no God.*

> • *Man makes his own heaven or hell on earth by his decisions.*

The big California earthquake rearranged my thinking about God. Now I was sure there was a Supreme Being, but who was He, She, or It? Judging that there must be a positive force and a negative force in the world, my assumption was that God was the positive force. I concluded, "If I can somehow plug into the right energy, I can accomplish anything!"

I began by reading a book entitled "The Power of the Subconscious Mind" which led me into metaphysical thinking. I started calling God "Divine Father." And the belief that I could tell Him my innermost desires and that He would jump to make my wishes come true gave me a great deal of peace. He was the first person I talked to in the morning and the last in the evening. Feeling protected and confident helped me decide to change my profession from secretary to salesperson.

My belief in the love of my "Divine Father" enhanced my success with Xerox, where I had just acquired a new sales position. I would walk into any customer's office quite assured that the president of the company had come that day just to meet with me. During this time, a gentleman had been given my name. He was a fellow-vegetarian and a successful producer with Motown Records. Someone thought we would make the perfect couple.

One afternoon, my sister and roommate, Elenor, looked up from the floor where she sat going through record albums and smiled, "Guess who I'm going out with tonight?" After guessing several potentials and watching her shake her head negatively to each suggestion, she finally said, "I'm going out with Frank Wilson."

Laughing, I responded, "I thought he was taking me out!"

Elenor smiled and said, "Yes, he was supposed to take you out. But because of your busy schedule, he could never catch you at home. So when he called today, he asked me what I was doing this evening. Knowing that you have more than enough dates, I accepted."

That was perfectly fine with me. Elenor was my best friend. I didn't even know this Frank Wilson, and I wholeheartedly hoped that they would have a wonderful time.

Frank was in the process of traveling back and forth to the east coast recording a new album and they had three dates over a four month period. She thought Frank was nice but the chemistry wasn't there. During this time she fell in love with someone else.

Meanwhile, Frank and I were becoming good friends. The relationship was strictly platonic. He had agreed to teach me how to play tennis and on many occasions we ended up at a local health food restaurant. My sister and I had never dated the same person. We both knew it could be detrimental to our relationship so I never gave Frank any personal consideration.

God's Timing

It was unusual for me to be at home on a beautiful Saturday afternoon, and the ringing telephone startled me. Standing beside the big picture window watching the newly budding tree just outside had caused me to ask myself a scientific question, "How does a tree know when to bloom and when to shed its leaves?"

The voice on the other end was warm and lively, "Hello, is Elenor there?"

I replied, "No, may I ask who's calling?"

"This is Frank." Elenor was out with her new love, so I was hoping he wouldn't ask me about her whereabouts. Instead we began talking about a variety of subjects. The thought crossed my mind, "This is a very interesting man."

Frank broke into my thoughts and asked, "So, Bunny, how is your love life?" A smile crossed my face as I sat up in my big soft livingroom chair. By now, I had become very active in metaphysical thinking. I responded with excitement, "I have a wonderful love life, Frank! There is someone in my life that is always there for me. He knows everything about me and yet still loves me. He protects, leads, and guides me. He is everything to me."

Today Frank says it was really difficult for him to hide his jealousy. He had always longed for that kind of love in his life. Trying to sound nonchalant, he asked, "Well, I know a lot of people in Hollywood. Maybe I know him. What is his name?"

Without hesitation I answered, "I don't know if you know him or not, Frank. It's God."

The silence on the other end was deafening. "Frank," I called. He mumbled a few words that neither of us remember and quickly ended the conversation. Little did I know, as I placed the telephone receiver down, that a button had been pushed in Frank's heart. Hanging up the phone, he recalled a recent conversation with his mother. She had been encouraging Frank to get married.

He'd responded, "Mom, I don't think I'll ever get married. Women are different today. It's important to me that whoever I marry loves God. And women like that just aren't out there." Those words echoed in his soul.

Frank had been raised in the church. He had no idea that the God I referred to had nothing to do with a personal relationship with Jesus Christ. A short time after that conversation, Frank asked me out on a date. With Elenor in love with someone else, she made it clear that my accepting a date with Frank was perfectly all right with her. But neither one of us realized or dreamed in our wildest imagination that four weeks later Frank Wilson would be my husband.

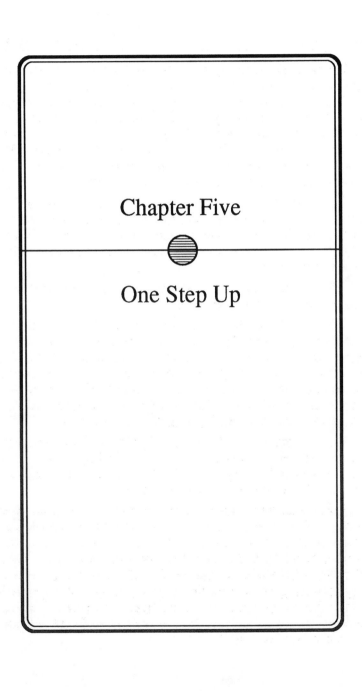

Chapter Five

One Step Up

Chapter Five

ONE STEP UP

My whirlwind romance with Frank swept me completely off my feet. It also swept away my "commitment of protection" never to get married. In many ways he reminded me of my father; successful yet humble, easygoing, and fun-loving. His award-winning smile captivated me. Best of all, he was one of the nicest people I had ever met. When he announced, "I believe the Lord wants you to be my wife," he received no resistance from me. I knew he was the one.

Our small private wedding was enchanting. The minister said that he had never before married a couple who kept their eyes closed throughout the whole ceremony! Neither of us was aware that the other's eyes were also closed. I remember concentrating on every word the minister said, meaning it with all my heart.

Once blissfully married, I packed my bags and moved to a new location; Frank's Hollywood Hills residence. I'm sure Bitterness loved its new surroundings when we arrived at our beautiful house, overlooking everywhere.

Our lives continued as usual. Frank was actively writing and producing pop music, and I was pursuing a successful sales career with Xerox Corporation.

Many nights found me asleep on the recording studio sofa while Frank worked around the clock meeting production deadlines. We were great friends and enjoyed each others' company. Then, a year later, there was a drastic turn of events in our lives.

A New Arrival

Frank's first wife, Barbara, had died when their daughter, Tracey, was just two years old. The girl was now ten years old and was being raised by Frank's mother in Houston, Texas. One day Frank announced, "I think it's time for Tracey to come and live with us. She's getting older and needs to be with her father."

There were no reservations in my heart. Considering how much I loved my father, I agreed with Frank. I thought, "Wow, this is going to be great. Tracey is going to come and we'll be one big happy family!" Looking back, I can see Bitterness rubbing its hands together in excitement. A large number of clocks were sitting on the fireplace mantel of my heart, and Bitterness had more than enough to work with in bringing havoc to our home.

Just three months before Tracey came to us, I asked Jesus Christ to be my Lord and Savior. I was introduced to the Lord at the Mt. Zion Missionary Baptist Church pastored by Dr. E. V. Hill. Frank had recommitted his life to the Lord, and we were attending church regularly. My new-found faith was exciting, and we immediately became actively involved in church activities.

Tracey arrived in August of 1974.

Frank and I stood at the airport gate waiting for the passengers to deplane, when we saw Tracey emerge between two tall men. Her baby doll was gripped tightly to her chest, and her big almond eyes reflected her excitement and anxiety of beginning a new life with her father and stepmother. My heart went out to her. I longed to take her in my arms and love her. But I didn't. A warm smile and a quick hug were all my clocks would allow me to do.

When Tracey looks back on her thoughts and feelings upon moving to Los Angeles, she says, "I was excited about moving to be with my father and new step-mother. She was pretty and I couldn't wait to comb her long hair. I just knew everything would be wonderful."

Unfortunately, within a few months Tracey was calling Houston regularly, begging her grandmother to please let her return. It's amazing to see how the two of us, having such high expectations for our relationship, so quickly came to a place of dislike and hostility.

An Ultimatum

Five years came and went; five years of living hell. It wasn't that Tracey was an unkind or unruly child. She was never disrespectful. It was just that her presence constantly demanded something of me that I couldn't provide. I didn't have warm embraces, kind words and encouragement to offer. They weren't given to me during my childhood, and now I didn't have them to give to Tracey.

My mother grew up in a cold, critical, and unloving environment. She had not been a villain, but a victim. Because she was a victim, I became a victim. And my condition destined Tracey to be a victim also. The love I so freely gave to Frank came naturally. It had been rehearsed consistently with my father throughout the years. But living with this child that I did not carry or birth was like living with an alien creature. What do you say? What do you do? I didn't have a positive role model, so I simply drew from my own experience: I criticized.

One night when Frank returned from the studio, I announced, "Tracey has to go! Either she goes or I go, but I can't live like this anymore!"

Frank was pensive as he answered, "You know Bunny, perhaps you should consider treating Tracey in a manner consistent with your teachings."

He didn't need to say anything else. His piercing words
shot through my body like a burning sword. Over the past
few years, Frank and I had been having Bible studies at
our home every other weekend and a hundred people
regularly attended. I was always quite vocal in speaking
about the love of Jesus Christ and encouraging everyone
to reach out and love one another. Almost every conversation, whether with friends or strangers, involved my telling them how they could become Christians and
experience God's love and plan for their lives.

It didn't take me long to conclude that in order for me
to continue proclaiming the love of God, I would have to
climb over Tracey. I disliked her, and she was living in
my own home. I tossed and turned all night long. Bitterness was taunting me on the one hand, and the Lord was
calling me to do right on the other. The next morning,
after Frank had left for the studio, I fell on my face before
the Lord and cried, "Lord, I hate her! I don't want her in
my house! I don't know how to love her. If you don't
remove these feelings from my heart, she'll have to go!"

After crying for what seemed an endless period of time,
I heard the voice of the Lord within saying, "Bunny, this
is what I want you to do. Starting today, I want you to
keep a journal of your relationship with Tracey. And here
are my first instructions: I want you to start praising her
three times a day."

Dying to Self

The instructions seemed simple enough. Although I
had not been keeping a journal, I obtained one that day
and began to document our relationship. The journal was
no problem; it was the second request that was torment-
ing me. For many people, saying something kind three
times a day would be a piece of cake. For me, it was like

speaking a foreign language.   Complimenting always sounded phony to me.

By afternoon I had not given Tracey one word of praise. Dinner was over, and I could hear her moving around in the kitchen. I remembered how many times I had admired the thoroughness with which she cleaned the kitchen. I could hear the sounds of dishes being rinsed. Hesitantly, uncomfortably, I walked into the room. Standing by the counter, it seemed as if a lifetime passed. I broke out into a cold sweat. My hands were wringing wet.

"Tracey," I finally said, "I just wanted to say that I think you do a great job cleaning the kitchen."

Tracey's face registered bewilderment as she looked over her shoulder at me. Once the words had been uttered, I quickly made my way back to the bedroom. I closed the door, threw myself across the bed, and cried for a long time. Complimenting my stepdaughter had been one of the hardest things I'd ever done!

A few hours later, I commented on how well she took telephone messages. I also mentioned that I was grateful I didn't have to remind her to practice the piano. I sighed with relief. My commitment to the Lord had been kept! But what in the world would I have to say tomorrow?

I soon discovered that when you look at a person through eyes of appreciation, the list of positives becomes never-ending.   Tracey quickly responded to my kind words. Complimenting her was like pouring water on a desert. She began to bloom almost immediately.

My journal began August 20, 1979. My entry nine days later read, "Our relationship has been steady. Very good at times, average at others, but it hasn't been poor since August 20th."

As I thumb through my writings, it seems almost impossible that just three weeks after I began praising Tracey I wrote, "Things are better than ever with Tracey. She has begun to do small things to help and, of course, I have been complimenting her. She is such a sweet person. I'm glad she's my daughter."

All of the entries in my journal were not happy ones. There were days when I was despondent and it seemed as if we were continuously taking "three steps forward and two steps back". One entry read, "Thank you, Lord, for the test of loving someone even when they don't seem to receive it."

During my years of service to Christ, this was the first time I was called to die to myself in such a critical area. My commitments of protection never to allow anyone to get close enough to hurt me had always kept me at arm's distance with Tracey. Dropping my guard was frightening. Fortunately, at the time I never dreamed that this was only the first step in what Jesus would eventually call me to do.

After observing many blended families, it is easy for me to see the source of many of their challenges. So many betrayals have usually taken place before the marriage, usually affecting both the husband and the wife.

Each comes into the relationship with a mantel full of clocks. Every one of those timepieces has frozen their emotions and actions. To make matters worse, children may have their share of clocks, too. They have probably come through at least one poor relationship and are suddenly entering the unknown.

It's no wonder that approximately 42% of first time marriages and a startling 67% of second time marriages end in divorce. With Bitterness at the helm and with marital partners frozen within their commitments of protection, relationships are often doomed to fail from the beginning. Forgiving and loving unconditionally all those involved in past hurts are key actions. They are absolutely necessary steps that must be taken before entering into another intimate association.

But what about my relationship with Tracey?

Six years after my first entry in the journal I wrote, "This past weekend I had the privilege of seeing Tracey marry David Hampton." The wedding was so beautiful! Tracey was an incredible example of a young woman who chose to get married in Jesus Christ.

Today, after persistently working through so many obstacles and misunderstandings, our relationship is better than ever. As well as being my daughter, Tracey is also one of my closest friends.

Thank you, Lord!

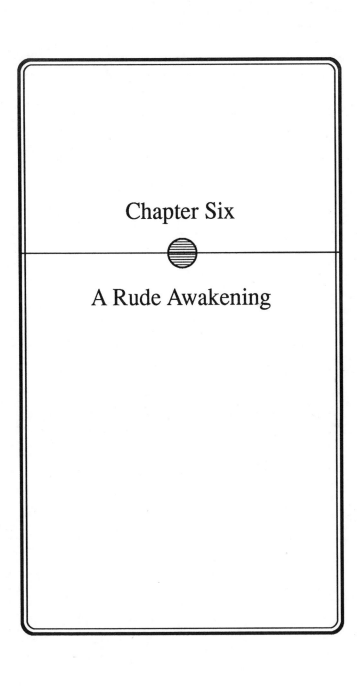

Chapter Six

A Rude Awakening

Chapter Six

A RUDE AWAKENING

If a show of hands were requested in answer to the question, "Who believes that God will not give you more than you can bear?" mine would be the first one up. My challenges with Tracey were emotionally difficult enough. Had I been forced to deal with my mother at the same time, it would have been more than I could have faced.

By the time Tracey was married, it was beginning to dawn on me that the Lord uses circumstances to get our attention. He doesn't allow difficulties to attack, discourage, or destroy us, but rather they shine a light on the dark places in our hearts. Jesus truly is the "Light of the World," and His "Light" is essential.

My pastor describes life this way, "You are usually in one of three places in life: You're going into a storm, you're in the middle of a storm, or you're coming out of a storm."

Mom and my little sister, Lizzie, moved to Los Angeles to be with Dad two months before my marriage to Frank. Mom and Dad's relationship lasted only a few months more. Unfortunately, they divorced, but for the first nine years following her arrival, there was not a harsh word between Mom and me. As far as my relationship with her was concerned, I had come out of the storm. Although there was little contact between us at first, a year after arriving in California, Mom became a Christian.

My excitement could not be contained when I thought of what that would mean to us and our mother/daughter friendship. Now that both of us had surrendered our lives to Christ, I believed "old things had passed away and, behold, everything had become new". I had chosen to forgive Mom of past hurts and, judging by her actions toward me, she had surely done the same.

I was in for a rude awakening.

After nine years, I went back into the storm. My desire to start fresh and begin building on a solid foundation had blinded me. Bitterness had no intention of giving up his territory. Perhaps if my "rose-colored glasses" had been removed, I might have recognized some obvious signs. But my glasses allowed me to see only a healthy relationship that grew stronger with each passing day. Regular telephone calls, consistent visits and the celebration of special days marked our fellowship.

My first child, Launi, heightened my appreciation for my mother. As the joys and challenges of motherhood were experienced for the first time, she was indispensable. My second and third daughters only served to deepen my gratitude.

After my mother had surgery, I was the only one of her children who was able to care for her. Cliff and Elenor (who had each married) lived out of state, and I was perfectly happy to travel to the hospital. Unhappy with the response of her friends to her bedridden state, I ordered several arrangements of flowers and wrote in names so that she would be encouraged. Making sure there was food prepared at her house and tending to her needs brought me joy.

One night at 3 a.m., a telephone call from Mom sent Frank and me scurrying to her home—a 45-minute drive. All she had said when the receiver was placed to my ear was, "Can you come?" I understood the distress she was experiencing over her divorce, and my heart went out to her. We took Mom and Lizzie home with us, and they stayed for three days before she felt strong enough to return home.

Victim Not Villian

Mother is one of the kindest people I have ever met. A poll of her neighbors would confirm that statement. They have all been the recipients of her tender loving care. If someone becomes ill, he'll get chicken soup delivered, whether he wants it or not. Many neighbors have been delightfully surprised to find flowers growing in their gardens, flowers that Mom had planted as a special surprise.

I've said it again and again - my mother is not a villain, she is a victim. And, like many of us, she allowed Bitterness to take root and ferment until finally it was ready to strike.

Heb. 12:15 warns, "Be careful that the root of bitterness be not found in you, lest it rise up and defile many." Bitterness carefully marks its time to "rise up." Years can pass without it surfacing. However, like a killer tornado, once it begins its assault, it menaces everything in its path. Had I been more observant, some ominous black clouds would have warned me.

The dark clouds first appeared when, as my children grew older, they came back home after spending the weekend with Grandma with a less-than-positive attitude. There always seemed to be a spirit of contention upon their return. I simply assumed it came from the excitement of having spent three days with someone they loved deeply.

One day Launi was working on a report for her tenth grade English class. The assignment was to write about the twelve most meaningful incidents in her life. In the twenty-five page report, which included two pages entitled, "Grandma's House," she wrote: "They say that grandmas spoil you rotten. Well, I know that mine dies, but she also provides discipline. This is an example of a day at Grandma's house..."

Launi proceeded to describe waking up to the smell of a delicious breakfast, getting ready to spend the entire day at the beach with her grandmother, sisters and cousins, eating dinner at a pizza parlor, and ending the day by playing card games and eating snacks. Grandma would always put the girls to bed with prayer. Launi ended her report by stating how important her grandmother was to her and by acknowledging the impact she'd had on her life. Her distress, and that of my other two children, was understandable when their visits to Grandma's house were abruptly halted in January of 1986.

Retribution

The decision to stop the visits with Grandma was not made overnight. Whenever my children returned after a weekend visit, they increasingly challenged my authority. There was a spirit of disrespect, subtle yet obvious. As I listened more closely to their statements, it began to dawn on me that Mom was beginning to plant Bitterness towards me in the hearts of my children. Often, when I attempted to discipline or correct them, they would quote something Grandma had said I had done as a child. These were not kind remembrances. And as far as my girls were concerned, they supposedly provided justification for their not doing what I asked them to do.

Knowing my mother, I doubt that she did any of this consciously. But while I was still living at home, she often said, "I hope when you grow up you have a daughter that treats you just the way you treat me!" My curt response always was, "When I grow up, if I have a daughter, she won't treat me the way I treat you. Because I won't treat her the way you treat me!"

This unpleasant and repeated exchange began to come back to me.

When we harbor bitterness in our hearts, we may be able to tolerate the presence of the person who betrayed us, but we don't want to see them blessed. We secretly hope that one day they'll be paid back for the way they hurt us.

My children love me. My efforts to go out of my way to make them feel loved, encouraged, and accepted had created a tremendous bond between us. But each weekend spent with their grandmother helped to remind them that maybe I wasn't so perfect after all.

While I was getting ready to back out of Mom's driveway one Sunday afternoon with the children in the car, she leaned over and said through the window, "I don't think you should teach your children to say 'Yes, sir' or 'No, Ma'am' to adults. A simple yes or no would do."

There are many people who might agree with her. However, this courtesy reflected a decision that my husband and I had made in the up-bringing of our children. And when Mom made that statement in the girls' presence, it was just one more way that she was again undermining my authority.

The Last Straw

One morning nine-year-old Fawn was standing in the middle of her bedroom, getting dressed for school. Observing the scanty look of her clothing, I said, "Fawn, that outfit is inappropriate for school. Please add something to it or change to another outfit."

Fawn put one hand on her hip and quipped, "I don't know why I have to change. Grandma said when you were growing up, you used to wear short-shorts with no panties!"

Bitterness laughed as the weight of those words struck like a cannon ball in my chest. I still felt shame about some of the ways I had conducted myself as a young girl. I responded angrily, "Did Grandma tell you that I wasn't a Christian? Did she tell you that she let me go out of the house like that?"

Turning quickly, I shouted over my shoulder, "You change those clothes young lady!"

That was the straw that broke the camel's back! I repeatedly asked myself, "Why would my mother discredit my Christian witness to my children?" I had always been open in testifying to adults about my past behavior, about the lifestyle the Lord had brought me from. But I knew that sharing those things with my children, who could not yet fully understand the circumstances, would be devastating. My mother had shared something with my daughters that I felt one would only tell an enemy's child.

Once the girls had left for school, I sat weeping on the end of my bed. Under my breath I said softly and incredulously, "She is still bitter. After all these good years and the wonderful things we have experienced together, she is still bitter!" I couldn't believe it.

I went to Frank for counsel. And my hand trembled as I wrote a letter to Mom explaining why the children would not be allowed to visit her any more. I cited the statements made by my children; I pointed out instances that appeared to be attempts on her part to weaken my parental authority and to plant Bitterness against me in the hearts of my children.

Knowing that Mom deeply loved her grandchildren, just as they loved her, I agonized over this decision. A few days later, I called to see if she had received the letter and to let her know that I wanted to talk about it. Her response was curt. Once I hung up the telephone, it would be nine months before Mom and I were to speak again.

Chapter Seven

The Showdown

Chapter Seven

THE SHOWDOWN

August 12, 1986 was to be a memorable day. The night before had found me tossing and turning relentlessly in my bed. As I described earlier, I was searching out how to know Christ. My time together with Him had left me with only one choice. If I wanted to experience deep and abiding fellowship with Christ, I was going to have to call Mom.

Before I had a chance to pick up the telephone and dial Mom's number, Tracey's husband, David, called. She was in labor with their first child at the birthing clinic! We rushed across town to be with her. It was my first participation in the birth of a child other than my own. Tracey smiled when we walked into the room. "Hi, Dad and Mom," she said. She was seated at the side of the bed with pain etched across her face. As it turned out, she had another three hours to go.

As the minutes ticked by and the pain grew more and more intense, the doctor encouraged her to bear down with the contractions. Once Tracey was in the final stage of labor, she was exhausted, "I can't do this! It hurts," she screamed.

The doctor urged her, "You CAN do it, Tracey. The baby should be here with one more push." As the next contraction began, Tracey pushed with her last ounce of strength and Robert Michael was born.

The Lord spoke clearly to me as I watched her next response. The baby was laid on her stomach, and as he cried, Tracey cooed softly, "It's o.k., baby. You're going to be all right. Mommy is here."

Gone was the agony of only seconds before! It was as if she had suffered no pain. The product of her suffering was worth all her anguish. Jesus whispered to me, "This is what it will be like as you work through your relationship with your mother."

The First Step

I called Mom from the hospital hallway. My hands were trembling as I pushed the buttons on the pay phone. My shakiness came both from what I had just seen and from what I was about to do. Mom answered on the other end of the line with her usual cheery voice.

"Hi, Mom, this is Bunny," I said hesitantly. She didn't seem surprised. "How are you?" she responded.

"I'm doing great! Tracey just had a baby boy," I replied. The baby became our focus as I described the events that had just taken place.

When the conversation began winding down, I drew up the courage to say, "Mom, I'd like to come and see you."

"Sure, that will be fine," she answered. Arrangements were made for me to go by that evening. After dropping Frank off at the airport for an out-of-town speaking engagement, I headed for Mom's house. I was in a panic. My hands were dripping and my stomach fluttered at every thought of our encounter. My instructions from the Lord were clear. "Bunny," He said, "I want you to go and listen. I will tell you what to say."

Mom's front yard was as beautiful as ever. She always spent countless hours tending her flowers. The walk to her front door was short but seemed to take an eternity.

She opened the door quickly and from the look on her face, it was as if no time had passed.

Leading me to her kitchen table, she immediately began to talk about the trip she had just taken to our hometown, Youngstown, Ohio. Glancing up at the kitchen clock, I noted that it was 7:00 p.m. Half an hour later, she was still laughing and sharing stories about people we knew and how the town had changed.

When she finally paused, I said, "You know, Mom, I was wondering about something on my way over here. Before we die, will we ever get to know one another?"

Her laughter fell silent. The smile left her face. She looked at me with the eyes of a dead person. "Never!" she emphatically answered. I was startled by her firmness.

"Never, Mom?" I questioned. "That means no way, no how, not a chance."

Mom rose quickly from the table and glared down at me angrily, "No, never!" she repeated, "I could never forgive you for the things that you have done to me."

Now I knew why the Lord had asked me to listen and to wait for Him to tell me what to say. This would have been the time when I would have run quickly to my mental files and pulled out my list of everything Mom had ever done to hurt me. We would have then gone tit-for-tat until one of us exploded.

"Mom," I said instead, "I came here tonight for two reasons. One, so that our relationship can be healed and two, so we can begin to learn how to love each other."

Again Mom answered, "That could never happen. You have done too much."

At that moment, the doorbell rang. Her fiance, Eddie, had arrived. He came in and sat down at the table across from us.

Memories

Eddie's presence seemed to bolster her resolve. Mom began to recount the past in detail. Her one-sided, graphic accounts cut into my soul as she painted a picture of an insensitive, selfish, evil child. I listened. At one point she stated, "I could never forgive you because when you were thirteen years old, you said that you hated me and wished I never was your mother!"

"Mom," I replied, "I was a child! I thought like a child. I don't feel that way about you anymore. I love you."

"No," she insisted. "I could never forgive you. It's like it happened yesterday. I can still hear those words ringing in my ears."

As she continued, it was as if I were looking into the face of Bitterness itself. Mom was speaking to me as though I were still a teenager, as if time had never moved. The clocks on her mantlepiece, frozen in the past, stood in defiance of change. I thought to myself, "What about the nine years we spent together without a harsh word between us? What about the times I was there for you when you needed me? Why don't you remember that?"

The Lord whispered softly into my soul, "All of the good things you did were applied to your bad account. You still came up owing!"

As Mom continued to spew out her hatred, anger and pain, I listened. Every now and then I would repeat, "Mom, I came here for two reasons; so our relationship could be healed and so we can learn to love one another."

By now Mom's words were beginning to frighten me. The depth of her root of bitterness was overwhelming. For the most part, it could not be detected with the human eye. For years her kindness and gentle ways had masked the hidden infected resentment she held in her heart.

Before the evening was over, I had to respond one more time to something she said when Mom announced, "You're the reason your father and I got a divorce!"

Stunned by the statement, I responded pleadingly, "Mom, you can't mean that! I was twenty-three years old when you and Dad got a divorce. I left home when I was seventeen. How could I possibly be responsible for your divorce?"

She replied, "Oh no, you're the reason. You were always your father's favorite child. When I would say 'No', he would say 'Yes.' Our worst arguments were over you!"

"But, Mom, you can't blame that on me. I was a child. I just wanted my way. He was the adult making the decision. How could that have been my fault?"

Mom convincingly replied, "You knew exactly what you were doing. You manipulated the whole thing!"

I sat in shock. She believed every word she was saying! No wonder she was discrediting me to my children. My mother loved my father and she was holding me responsible for the destruction of their marriage.

At this point, I remembered conversations with my father which provided me with his perspective of their difficulties. I knew there was more to the story than this, but it still devastated me to hear my mother's words.

Over three hours had passed, and Mom was just as adamant as when we began. By now she had completely destroyed anything positive about my character or reputation. Between the accusations and the profanity, I was entering into the last phase of my contractions of pain. I knew I couldn't take any more.

As I stated once again the reason for my presence, Mom angrily cast the offer for reconciliation aside.

Eddie, who was deeply in love with her and sympathized with her pain, placed his hand on top of hers and said, "For God's sake, Liz, listen to the child. She's trying to make it right by you!"

Mom turned her indignant gaze on him and spurted, "Oh yeah, it's easy for you to say. I guess if your daughter walked in here tonight, you would forgive her for what she's done to you. Not a chance!"

The reminder of the bitterness he held in his own heart silenced his pleas.

The clock in the kitchen said it was 11:30 p.m. Nearly four hours had passed; hours of deep rejection and unrelenting insults. Bitterness was laughing hysterically. It hissed, "I told you not to come! You should have listened to me."

With a deep sigh, I turned to my mother and said, "Mom, I have to go. I came here for two reasons, to see our relationship healed and to learn how to love you. What do you want to do? Can we agree just to begin? To start out fresh? The ball is in your court, Mom. What do you want to do?"

Mom studied her folded hands on the table for what seemed a lifetime. When she looked up, her gray eyes seemingly covered with ice, she responded slowly, "If I had to do it all over again, I never would have had you!"

The whining of Bitterness grew deafening as it reached into its bag of clocks to place one on the fireplace of my heart. This was the biggest clock ever added to my collection. It looked extremely large as it sat alone on my mantel. The other clocks, with the help of the Lord, had been cleared away.

Blinded by tears, I quickly fumbled around for my purse. Racing for the front door, the keys to my car which had fit when I came to her house, somehow wouldn't go into the lock. Finally, I opened the door, started the engine, backed out of my mother's driveway and headed up the street. I wiped my tears away with the back of my hand and shouted to the Lord, "How could she say that! How could she say that she's sorry she ever had me? Does that mean that my life has been good for nothing?"

Silence was my answer. Repeating the words I heard Tracey say earlier that morning, I angrily announced, "I can't do this! It hurts!"

I don't know if Jesus responded; I wasn't open to listening. Thinking I was able to know Him in the "fellowship in his sufferings" had been a mistake. I would have to be content to socialize with Jesus for the rest of my life. The cost of fellowship was too high.

Pity Party

I cried for what turned out to be three days. I felt no desire to pray or talk to the Lord because I wasn't interested in what He had to say. The depth of rejection from my mother was inexpressible.

Despondent, depressed, and discouraged, I thought about how I had been a speaker at women's conferences and churches for the past ten years and how so many people had told me that the Lord had used me to change their lives. Now here I was in the pit of despair, not knowing the way out.

I shared with Frank over the telephone what had happened in my time with Mom. The Lord used him to minister to me because I had shut down all lines of communication between myself and Jesus. I sobbed into the phone and cried, "I don't know what to do!"

Frank replied, "You have to love her, Bunny, with unconditional love. Treat her as if nothing happened. Just love her."

When I hung up, I knew that was exactly what the Lord had done for me. Jesus "looked beyond my faults and saw my needs." Even when I was still an enemy of the cross,

Christ had died for me. For the first time, I had a taste of the terrible suffering He had experienced to give me eternal life.

He too had "just listened" when He was brought before the Sanhedrin Council before His crucifixion, and He had done absolutely nothing wrong! Some of the things Mom had said about me had been true. I began to appreciate how Jesus must have felt after living His life perfectly, doing nothing but good, yet being falsely accused.

I thought about Luke 6:35-36:

> "But love your enemies, do good and lend, expecting nothing in return. For even your Father is kind to the ungrateful and unthankful. Therefore, even as your Father is merciful, be ye merciful."

An enemy is a person who goes out of his way to mess up our day—someone who cheers when bad things happen to us. Yet here God is calling us to love our enemies and to expect nothing in return. This is unconditional love—exactly the kind of love that Frank had exhorted me to give to my mother.

As I sat weeping by the telephone, Jesus spoke clearly, "Bunny, if you love Me, you will keep My commandments, the Father will love you, and I and the Father will come and abide in you." I knew it was His voice. I could look up the words for myself in John 15:23.

Knowing Him

Once again, I asked Jesus, "What do you want me to do?"

He answered, "I want you to tell your mother that you love her, and from today on, I want you to love her unconditionally. Look for nothing in return."

Bitterness thought the suggestion was absurd and grabbed from the mantel the large clock whose betrayal time was frozen to 11:30 p.m., August 12, 1986.

Shaking the clock in my face, it taunted, "You're a glutton for punishment! Haven't you had enough?"

All at once, righteous indignation ignited within me. I reached up and grabbed Bitterness by the neck and pulled its green slimy body down on my lap. Holding it firmly with one hand, I dialed my mother's number with the other. When she answered the phone, I shakily said, "Hi, Mom, this is Bunny. I don't have long to talk, but I just called to say I love you." A few short words later I hung up the telephone.

Bitterness screamed and dropped the clock. I heard the glass break. The clock began to tick and the hands began to move.

No longer would I be frozen in my bitterness towards Mom. It would not be enough to say that I forgave her. Jesus was calling me to love the one who had betrayed me with unconditional love. I began to understand that if I did it for nothing in return, Bitterness would have to throw its bag of clocks away. My trust and hope was now in Christ, not in man or woman.

Now I understood what Jesus meant when he said he was betrayed by His disciples, but He forgave them and loved them. He didn't hold it against them. I had decided to align myself with His Word which says, "Let this mind be in you which was also in Christ Jesus."

My late-night conversation with Jesus came to mind. I recalled his instructions about how I could know Him, and these thoughts reawakened my desire to talk to Him. I suddenly missed Him! Once we have experienced a one-on-one fellowship with Christ, no relationship can compare. No one on earth can provide such peace and love.

The Right Step

Even though I was determined to expect "nothing in return" from Mom, the first few times I called her were difficult. Old habits die hard. However, little by little, liberation came through obedience. I knew when I called that she didn't want to talk to me. If she wasn't in and I left a message, I already knew there would be no return phone call. It would be a year-and-a-half before she returned one of my messages.

Nevertheless, I checked on Mom every week. I sent cards of love and appreciation on a regular basis. When she did speak to me and the conversation took a turn toward a confrontational subject, I steered it in another direction. I wasn't in her life to fight, I was there to love! On several occasions, Mom said things that were cutting and unkind, but for the first time in my life, her words were losing their destructive impact.

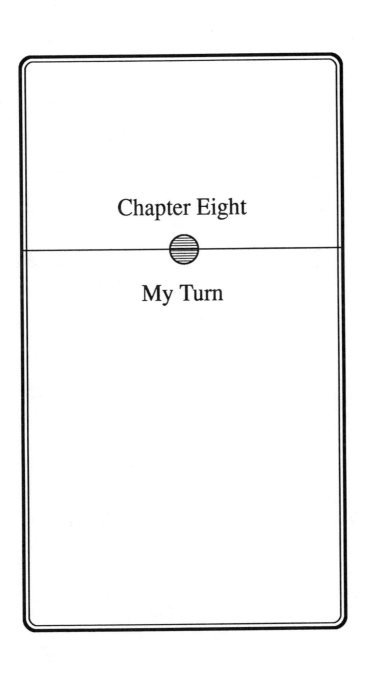

Chapter Eight

My Turn

Chapter Eight

MY TURN

Summer vacation was to begin in a week. Launi marched onto our back porch where I was sitting at the patio table and informed me, "I've decided what I'm going to do for the summer. First, I'll spend a week at Grandma's house and then go to..."

Cutting her off in the middle of her announcement, I said, "Launi, you will not be going to your grandmother's house for a week. I'll take you over to visit for the day, but you won't be spending the night."

"Why?" shouted Launi. "Why are you keeping us from Grandma? I love her!"

With that statement, Launi turned on her heel and stomped away. Calling Frank at his office, I recounted my conversation with Launi. Frank asked, "How much do they know?"

"They don't know anything. I haven't told them."

"I think," Frank suggested, "that it's time to tell them the truth."

Fortunately the children had just started school when I cut off their trips to Grandma. The demand of their school schedules, busy weekends seemed to have distracted their attention away from Grandma. When they mentioned visiting, I would just smile and say, "Maybe".

Rounding up Launi, Fawn, and Christy, I asked them to have a seat on the living room sofa. I sat down across from them and began, "A year ago, I wrote Grandma a letter and told her that you would not be allowed to visit anymore. I made that decision when I realized that she was still bitter towards me about some things that happened between us when I was a child. I became concerned when I realized through her comments that the bitterness she felt for me was being passed on to you."

My nine-year-old daughter, Fawn, shifted in her seat, let out a deep sigh and crossed her arms in a show of disgust.

I continued, "Your grandmother is not a villain, she is a victim. And because she is a victim, I became a victim. It's my job to make sure that doesn't happen to you. I don't believe that Grandma had been unkind on purpose. I think she's hurt, and her hurt began to show up in things she said to you.

"I love your grandmother and am working hard to see her healed of bitterness. I want to have a healthy relationship with her. But it's going to take time and I need to ask for your patience."

Without changing her position, Fawn responded in her usual analytical tone, "Mother, let's be honest. The reason we can't see Grandma is because you are bitter. And because you are bitter we are being kept from seeing someone we really love!"

I shudder to think what my response would have been to Fawn if a year of unconditional love had not been invested in Mom. Surely I would have put her impudent behavior in its place, only deepening her resolve. But fortunately I was fellowshipping with Christ and could hear His voice clearly. I silently asked Him to give me wisdom.

"Fawn," I said, "I want you to be the judge. For over a year, I have been calling Grandma weekly. You've overheard our conversations because many times you've been in the room with me. You have heard me tell her how much I appreciate her. In this past year, have you ever known Grandma to call me?"

There was no response from Fawn. I continued, "Also, you have seen me mail many cards to Grandma which express my love and commitment. Some of them you even read over my shoulder as I was writing. Have I recevied any cards from Grandma?"

Fawn sat in silence.

"Just a few weeks ago, Fawn," I reminded her, "I piled all of you into my car, drove 45 minutes to Grandma's house and we shared with her our gifts for Mother's Day. Then I went around the room and had each of you say something special about her. When it came to my turn, I expressed how I was sorry that she was hurt in the past but that I deeply love and care for her. Have I received any special presents over this past year from Grandma?"

I rushed to say, "Fawn, based on the facts, which one of us really is bitter?" Fawn shrugged her shoulders. But the mere fact that she didn't have a quick response indicated that she was considering my statements.

This conversation demonstrates how Bitterness usually passes the torch from one generation to the next. If I had not been loving Mom unconditionally, I would have stood accused by my children. They would have been angry towards me and turned their affections to Mom. Consequently the negative statements she had made to them about me in the past would have rung true in their hearts.

Because of my fellowship with Jesus, Bitterness had lost again. Unconditional love had vindicated me.

A few months later, Fawn was helping me cook in the kitchen. We began talking about some of her grandmother's favorite dishes. Fawn said nonchalantly, "Boy, Grandma may be bitter, but she sure can cook."

Smiling, with my back to Fawn, I thanked the Lord for showing her the truth. Bitterness had been stopped from flowing to my children through their grandmother. But the battle wasn't over.

Now it was my turn.

Facts Don't Count

I have always felt a special sensitivity towards my middle child, Fawn. I know that middle children often get lost in the shuffle, and I've gone out of my way to let her know she is special. Even though she was the second born, many times I would hold her and let her know that she was "second to none." Unfortunately, my efforts seemed to have little impact on Fawn.

Watching her personality characteristics and attitudes develop was like looking in a mirror. She had a strong pessimistic viewpoint. Her comments were often curt and unkind. Up to thirteen, she never had a teacher she liked and I'd spent a great deal of time at school trying to be a liaison between her and her instructors. In spite of our similarities, I was bewildered by her attitude. She had been the recipient of what I ached for as a child: affection, attention, love, and encouragement. Yet none of these things seemed to make a dent in her cynicism.

When adults met Fawn for the first time, they often commented that she was withdrawn and distant. Being her mother, I saw a side of her that few people knew. Fawn is the most compassionate of all my children.

If someone is in need, Fawn is available to help. She's always loved animals and babies but has had a low tolerance for people. Sometimes when she accompanied me to social gatherings, I would say to her as we approached the door, "Now, Fawn when we get inside, I want you to treat these people like dogs." I knew that if she treated them like dogs, they would receive a warm reception.

In those days, Fawn could walk around the house with a smirk on her face for three days straight. Nothing I would say or do would change her attitude, and I found this stubbornness quite annoying. Furthermore, I became increasingly concerned when in junior high school she befriended some girls of questionable character. Her grades were low. Teachers were constantly upset by Fawn's attitude and actions in the classroom.

Coming To A Head

On the third day of one of Fawn's attitude attacks, there was a misunderstanding as to a change in our travel schedule. She thought I would make a couple of stops before taking her to school one morning, because she had a strong aversion to arriving at school early. My plans called for dropping her off first. When she noticed that I was in the exit lane for her school, she shouted, "Where are you going? You're getting off on my exit!"

I quietly explained that she had misunderstood. As I drove down the exit ramp and began to slow down, Fawn placed her hand on the door handle, and ordered, "Just stop the car! I'm going to walk home and ask Dad to take me to school."

Three days of her bad attitude and now this ridiculous statement! I swung my right hand across the front seat with force, and the back of it landed squarely on her left arm. She screamed in pain. I brought the car to a stop and said, "Fawn, I'm sorry. I didn't mean to hit you in anger. Please forgive me."

As I drove up to her school, she jumped out of the car and slammed the door. That evening as she sat watching T.V. in our bedroom, she turned to Frank and said, "Did Mom tell you what she did to me today?"

Although I had told Frank, he looked up from his newspaper and asked, "What did she do?"

Fawn replied, "She hit me for no reason!"

Frank responded, "Oh, I'm sure she had a reason!"

Fawn shook her head emphatically.

I let the comment go uncontested but promised myself to have a discussion with Fawn. That took place three days later when we were alone, walking to Frank's office.

"Fawn," I said. "Do you remember the other day when you said that I hit you for no reason?" She nodded her head.

I continued, "Do you really think that you did nothing? What about your poor attitude which had been going on for three days? What about the absurdity of your actions that morning in the car?"

Fawn answered, "I didn't do anything. You were stressed and struck out at me for no reason."

I was speechless. In Frank's office, Fawn and I sat down at his conference table. I asked him to join us and I shared Fawn's most recent comments. Frank made a couple of remarks, only to be interrupted by a phone call. After he left, Fawn looked at me with defiance and said, "You hit me and that was wrong. If I hit you back, that would be wrong too. So I don't see why I can't hit you if you hit me!"

It felt as if someone had pulled a plug and all the air was being drained out of my body. Looking at Fawn was like looking at myself when I had struck my own mother at thirteen. I considered all the things that I had done for Fawn, only to have arrived in the same place. Despair overwhelmed me. What was the common denominator between us? The answer was rebellion and anger. But why?

I grabbed my coat and walked across the parking lot towards my car, not realizing that Frank was watching. He told me later that it looked as if I were carrying the weight of the world on my shoulders. As I moved across the parking lot, I knew I was about to make a decision. I was about to emotionally shut down on Fawn. Everything inside of me shouted, "Just give up! You've done all you can do. She has five more years at home and then she will be on her own. Just hang in there and take each day one day at a time. You have to let go or this will destroy you." This decision meant that I would physically be there, but I would not allow myself to be emotionally hurt by her again.

Then the Corinthian chapter on love came to mind. "Love bears all things, hopes all things, believes all things, endures all things....Love never fails."

No, I decided, I will not shut down on Fawn. I'm going to see this through.

That same evening Frank turned off his Monday football game and called a family meeting in the breakfast room. I had not told him about what Fawn had said about hitting me. I was quite surprised that he would miss his football to have a meeting.

Frank began by saying, "This family is in a crisis." Looking at our three daughters, he asked, "Do you know why this family is in a crisis?"

Launi, Fawn, and Christy had blank faces. As he questioned them individually, they struggled to come up with the proper answer. They went through the usual list of things: Not cleaning up their room. Not helping around the house. Having too many spats among themselves. Not being diligent in school.

Frank informed them, "This family is in a crisis because of the way you are treating your mother. I have noticed that there has been a decline in respect towards her and I will not tolerate it. I expect you to be obedient, helpful and courteous.

I had been staring at the floor, still numb from my confrontation with Fawn. As I looked up at Frank, he said, "I want each of you to go over to Mom, lay your hands on her and pray for her." Launi was first and Christy followed. Fawn walked hesitantly towards me, lightly placing her hand on my shoulder. "Lord," she mumbled, "Please make my mother..."

Frank stopped Fawn in the middle of her prayer and said, "Fawn, I told you to pray *for* your mother, not about her."

As Fawn began to pray for me, a dam of tears spilled from my eyes. My tears were of relief and conviction. I realized that in the past years of loving Mom unconditionally, I had never come close to understanding how she must have felt. I wondered what my response would have been if, in all my despair, Frank had come to me and said, "Why don't you get off Fawn's back!" I would have been devastated.

Now, for the first time, I felt the depth of Mom's pain throughout the years that Dad had continued to side with me. God was allowing me to empathize with her. My appreciation for her strength soared.

That evening I wrote her a letter and shared my experience with Fawn. At the end my words were, "You know, Mom, I don't think any of your children could love you as much as I love you because you have forgiven me more. I have told you many times that I was sorry for the pain I caused you. But this time, I want you to know that I'm sorry *and* that I understand."

During a phone call a few days later, Mom told me that she cried when she read the letter. She said, "All of my life, the only thing I wanted was to be understood. No one seemed to understand my pain. Your letter meant a lot to me."

As I hung up the telephone, I knew that God had allowed that incident to happen with Fawn so that I could understand Mom's pain. Through unconditional love, God was helping me to see the whole picture.

Love Never Fails

There would be other hurdles to jump during the process of helping Fawn overcome her rebellion and anger. Fortunately, I was committed to going all the way. The first hurdle came when I received a call from Fawn's school asking me to come pick her up. They were putting her out because she had started a protest to get a teacher reinstated that they had fired for a good cause. "Mrs. Wilson," the superintendent said, "I know there are only three weeks left before Fawn graduates from junior high school. However, she has been a considerable problem and since she's attending this school on permit, I must ask you to remove her and enroll her in another school. Please don't try to convince us to keep her. We've made up our minds."

When I went to the administration office to get Fawn's papers for her removal, a young lady looked up from her desk and said, "Aren't you Bunny Wilson? I heard you speak recently at a Christian growth conference."

My only regret was there was no trap door for me to escape. Seeing my embarrassment, she said, "Don't worry, Mrs. Wilson. 'All things work together for good for those that love the Lord.'" With a smile of appreciation, I left the room.

A few days later, Fawn ran away from home. We found her that evening at a friend's home. Frank and

I individually date our children so that we can spend
quality time with them, and instead of confronting her
then, I decided to wait for our date two days later to address the situation.

Taking Fawn to a poem reading at U.C.L.A., you could
cut the silence with a knife. On the way back, I asked,
"Fawn, what is really bothering you? Your father and I
love each other, we spend a lot of time with you and we
deeply care about you."

Fawn shrugged her shoulders and looked out her window. "Fawn", I said, "please don't shut down on me. Tell
me what is bothering you."

Fawn stated, "You're smothering us!"

"What do you mean?" I questioned.

"Everything we do has something to do with the Bible.
I don't even know if I believe in the Bible. I don't know
if I want to be a Christian!"

Fawn paused for a moment and said, "You and Dad
believe everything written in the Bible. What if it's a book
that a bunch of men made up? You're living your whole
life around it and because I'm your child, I'm forced to
do the same thing!"

It was easy to see how Bitterness would step into a conversation like this. Bitterness would remind me of all the
sacrifices made on Fawn's behalf. How I had tried to undo
everything my mother had done to make me miserable and
it appeared to all be for nothing. If I had allowed Bitterness to remain in my heart, my response to Fawn would
have been harsh as I reminded her of how fortunate she
was to have all the things I missed as a child. I would
have discounted her concerns and vented my frustrations
on her ungratefulness. It was a perfect set-up.

I prayed a silent prayer to God and asked Him for wisdom in my answer. "Fawn," I responded, "If you never

read the Bible, I would still love you. If you never become a Christian, I still love you. I don't love you because ..., I just love you."

When I glanced at Fawn, I noticed large tears rolling down her face. God knew that this was what Fawn needed to hear. My love for her was unconditional.

"Fawn," I continued, "I left home when I was seventeen years old, rebellious and angry, but I had a skill. If you leave home now, it would be dangerous because you have no way to take care of yourself. I have just one request to make. I know you love me. There are too many things you do in between the times you're angry that shows your love. Since you love me, Fawn, let me find a place for you to go where you can be happy and protected. I love you enough to let you go." By now, both of us were crying. The next morning, I could tell that Fawn was a different person. Her attitudes would flair up every now and then but not with the same consistency and definitely not the same intensity. Once again, unconditional love had won another victory and Bitterness was rendered helpless in destroying our relationship.

Two years later, Fawn committed her life to Christ. Her grades and conduct in school became exemplary. A smile crossed my face when she said one day, "Mommy, one of my friends at school said I love you too much. She thinks it sounds strange for someone in high school to call their mother "Mommy" and that's because I talk about you all the time.

I thought again about what Mom often said, "I hope you have a daughter that treats you just like you treat me."

Mom's hopes had come true, but thanks be unto God, love, not Bitterness, was there to greet her.

Chapter Nine

Putting An Axe to the Root

Chapter Nine

PUTTING AN AXE TO THE ROOT

The billowy white clouds outside the jumbo jet window were a visible representation of the soft peace felt in my soul. Looking to my left, I saw that Mom had fallen into a deep sleep. I reminisced over the past four years of loving her unconditionally. It had not been easy. When we take the steps to destroy bitterness in our lives, many times the person who has hurt us has not taken that same road.

Wanting to know Chirst more than wanting to hold onto my right to be bitter had guided me to "fellowship in His suffering", but it also allowed me to experience the "power of His resurrection". That power had raised Christ from the dead completely whole and yet it allowed His scars to remain. The scars of my past could be seen clearly in my testimony. When opportunities arose for me to share how God had set me free of bitterness, it was necessary for me to reveal the hurts of the past, but miraculously, there was no pain. Mom could press on those scarred areas with cutting remarks or an off-the-cuff joke, but the wounds had been healed.

The only reaction to pressure in the area of my wounds was unconditional love.

I believe that dying to ourselves so Christ can live out His fullness in us will be our ultimate test on earth. It's much easier to clothe the poor, feed the hungry, be faithful in the works of our local church, and visit those in prison. We can do those things with or without Christ, and although we are also called to participate in such ministries, I believe Jesus summed it up when He said: "If you would be My disciples, you must deny yourself, pick up your cross and follow Me."

Paul emphasized this point when he said, "I am crucified with Christ, nevertheless I live, yet not I, but Christ lives in Me."

An All-Expense Paid Trip

Mom and I were on our way to her homeland, Germany. She had promised each of her children an all-expense-paid visit to her country and our relatives. She had taken Cliff and then my baby sister, Elenor. Lizzie, who is now blind from the large amount of medication taken over the years, would not be making the long, arduous journey. Although she had promised to take each of us, nevertheless I was surprised when she finally invited me to go.

For the first time in our lives, we would be alone together with nothing but quality time. I was looking forward to introducing Mom to a daughter she didn't really know.

Anxiety could be heard in my brother's voice when we discussed the fact that I would be spending eight days alone with Mom. Having lived on the east coast for many years, he had not been an eyewitness to what God had done in our relationship. His recollections of me and Mom together were hostile and many times verbally violent.

I assured Cliff that the trip would be pleasant and fruitful. In my heart were two definite resolutions. One was that there was nothing that Mom could say or do to make me disrespect her in any way. God's Word commands us to "honor your father and mother". The other was to allow the Lord to minister to us in any way He chose.

Shortly after Mom awakened from her sleep, she was once again rehearsing the past. Bitterness imprisons and forbids us to move forward with our lives. As she shared her memories, my attention was riveted on every word. It was as if I were hearing the story of her disappointments with my father, the challenges of caring for a mentally retarded child, and her tragic childhood experiences for the first time. I ached for Mom and deeply longed for her to be free from all her unhappy yesterdays.

After two years of unconditionally loving Mom, some of the pieces of the puzzle began to fit together. My choice to love her out of obedience to Christ set me free, and the need to understand how we hurt one another became unimportant. However, Jesus wanted me to know. Through numerous conversations, the root of bitterness in our family tree became exposed.

Omah (grandmother in German) had visited us only a couple of times during my childhood. She was not the kind of person children would want to spend time with. Her cold grey eyes seemed to look right through us all.

I asked Mom about Omah's life. She said, "Omah had a hard time. Her mother died when she was nine years old and left her 750 pieces of gold. Her father remarried but her new stepmother hated her. When her father died, Omah, who was twelve, was sent to a work farm. She wasn't paid any money for her labor; it only took care of her room and board.

"Although it was difficult, the one thing that got her through was the 750 pieces of gold she had waiting for her when she turned eighteen. She planned to start her own business and put her ugly past behind her. When she turned eighteen, she discovered that somehow the 750 pieces of gold had been stolen and spent. She had nothing."

Later, when Omah had grown old, she came to pay Mom a yearly visit in Los Angeles. In her eighties, she would go for a walk every morning and then lay out in the sun on a lounge chair in the backyard. It was always startling to see her jump from a relaxed position only to begin arguing with an imaginary person. There was such hatred and anger in her expressions and body language! No one knew who it was she was arguing with, but that invisible person was as real to her as any of us.

Omah had been betrayed. It was easy, just by watching her lifestyle, to identify the clocks on her mantel and the "commitments of protection" she had made. When she lost the 750 pieces of gold, her commitment was that she would never be without money again. And she wasn't. She died wealthy because she refused to spend money even on necessary items.

When she was sent to that work farm, her commitment to "never force my child to work for her upkeep," could be seen in her faithful commitment to send funds to take care of Mom. She sent the money even though Mom was in an orphanage.

Omah was twenty-eight when she had Mom out of wedlock. In 1927 it was an utter disgrace to have a child without being married. There were no day care centers, and as Mom grew older it was difficult finding someone who would help. Omah knew she could find work in Switzerland, so she put my mother in an orphanage where she could be provided for while she worked. It seemed the reasonable thing to do. But as a child, Mom couldn't understand why she had a father but didn't have a father—why she had a mother but didn't have a mother.

My mother's clocks were easily recognizable also. There was no way she could feel appreciation for being in an orphanage. She had not lived through the agony of a work farm. All she knew was that she was betrayed and left by her mother. Her "commitment of protection" was,

"If I ever have children, they will have a father to help raise them."

I have come to understand that sometimes commitments are good but they are not good enough. Sometimes we go out of our way to make our children's lives better than our own. Yet there is no way they can understand and appreciate our actions. Many times a child will appear to be ungrateful, and this can cause anger and bitterness to arise in the parent. Even though we have tried to undo the bitterness of our past, it continues to pass to each generation in different forms until we decide to lay an ax to the root.

When at last we make the decision, we have to pay the price: unconditional love.

Unforgettable Experience

Germany met us with sunshine and a dramatic display of magnificent scenery. The little town of Kirchseon, a twenty minute train ride from Munich, rested lazily in the bright afternoon sun. As we drove along the quiet streets, I felt as if I were in a living art gallery with each scene more beautiful than the last. Acres of lush green grass surrounded storybook houses, every one nestled among trees. Each house had a balcony with lively red geraniums hanging from its flower boxes. Black and white cows strolled along the road side, all moving lazily in the same direction.

"Bunny!" said my godmother, Philomina, as she swung open her front door. "It's so wonderful to see you!" After kisses and hugs, I was seated in her country kitchen with a large spread of fresh bread, cheeses and cold cuts. This woman, with warm, dancing eyes, was my mother's best friend. I had been named after her and had been longing to ask her a question: "How did you get your name and what does it mean?"

"Philomina is a French name," she answered. "It was my mother's and grandmother's name. But I have no idea what it means". I had only been in Germany an hour and already I was delighted to know that my name had traveled through four generations.

We were soon joined by Philomina's (or Mina as she is affectionately called) children and it was delightful to watch the affection and closeness they felt for one another. A day didn't pass that my godmother did not break bread with one of her children or grandchildren.

Fascinated with history, I couldn't wait to walk the streets of Kirchseon and let Mom point out the many places she had often described to me. Mom posed for a picture beside the window of the house where my brother had been born. As we walked towards the railway station, Mom assured me that it looked exactly the same way it did when Dad used to catch the train from the army head-quarters and travel to see her. This time when she told me about her and Dad's first meeting, the story took on a special significance.

"It was a beautiful warm day in Munich," Mom recounted. "I missed my train and decided to walk home. As I was about to cross a small bridge, I noticed an American G.I. sitting on a large rock. He said in German, 'Good day, young lady' but I didn't stop walking. It was a disgrace in those days to speak to an American. Many of our fathers, brothers, and uncles were returning from the war wounded, crippled and dead after fighting with Americans. As I glanced out of the corner of my eye, his electrifying smile caught my attention. I was also fascinated by his dark skin. He was the first African-American I had ever seen." She paused to chuckle.

"To my dismay," she continued, "he climbed down off the rock and began to walk beside me. I said firmly under my breath, 'Go away!'"

"Well," she smiled, "he never went away. I fell in love with a warmhearted, funny and ambitious young man. He would take the train to Kirchseon every weekend to visit me."

Walking arm-in-arm with Mina, Mom said, "Your god-mother accepted him right away. She would walk from the train station with us. She didn't care that people stared, and I didn't care either. During those days, in spite of Hitler's outrageous agenda for a super race, racial issues in Germany were not important to the common people.

"We didn't even know what racism was, but my German countrymen hated the fact that I was dating the enemy, an American." She pointed to a sign above the railway station and remembered, "This is where your father first kissed me."

Mom smiled momentarily and then looked in the other direction.

I asked, "How long did it take before you got married?"

Mom frowned and said, "Too long! The Germans and Americans did everything to keep us apart. They threw me into jail for two months, but even that didn't stop us. We were walking down a road together one day and an American military officer that knew your father pulled up alongside us. He asked if we had gotten married yet. We explained how our papers kept getting lost. 'Jump in,' he said, and he took us to headquarters where he walked our papers through."

Mom paused in front of a four story building. She pointed to a window on the third floor. "Up there is where we had our party after the wedding. In those days everything was bought on the black market. People were amazed at the amount of food and drink we had."

Mom turned and looked across the street to a small apartment situated above a store. "That's where I lived with your brother Cliff after he was born."

The three of us, Mom, Mina, and I, continued arm-in-arm along the narrow streets. We were walking along the same small roads, across the same broken sidewalks that Mom and Dad had walked. They had been so in love, so filled with hope for their future. Our walk ended at a warm family restaurant where we filled up on some good German home cooking.

A Special Time

The clock said 2 a.m. and I noticed that Mom was not asleep on her side of the bed. Lying awake, I heard the voice of the Lord urging me to go and see about her.

I rounded the corner to the kitchen and saw Mom sitting at the table as white as a ghost. Whatever Mom had eaten that evening had not agreed with her system, or perhaps she had eaten too much of the deliciously rich food. Before I could offer my help, Mom quickly jumped up and ran towards the bathroom. She was soon quite sick, and I placed my hand on her back and began to silently pray. Mom was completely vulnerable, and the Lord had awakened me to minister to her.

I finally was able to help her to the breakfast room table, where she sat, visibly shaken by her ordeal.

Slowly the color began to return to her face as her system stabilized. It was too soon to return to bed, so we sat over cups of hot tea just talking. The conversation turned to Fawn and the challenges I had been facing. "You're fortunate," said Mom, "to know how to handle Fawn."

"Well, Mom, I've had good practice. She is just like I was when I was growing up. I know how she thinks, and rather than being angry that she is the way she is, I continuously ask God to show me how to redirect her negative energies so that she can become positive."

The next words out of my mouth came from an un-traveled path of logic. I knew the Lord was showing me a side of my mother I had never seen before. I said, "You know, Mom, you grew up in an orphanage. Your mother was not around. You never experienced a mother/daughter relationship. There was no way for you to relate to how you would have felt towards your mother as a teenager because you were not afforded that opportunity. It must have been very difficult dealing with teenagers when you had absolutely no reference point."

"Yes, it was," Mom quietly responded. "But it's just as well. It would have been difficult living with my mother. She was cold and mean."

Based on my mother's temperament, I was sure her ex-periences with her mother would have been much the same as mine with her. However, she never had an opportunity to find out. As a mother, she had no idea of the trials faced between parents and their children. Her time in the or-phanage left her with unrealistic dreams about the relation-ship she would have one day with her children.

As I climbed back into bed an hour later, I thought about how hard my mother's life had been. She came to the United States with my father. Six months later, he was called to return to Germany and she saw him only inter-mittently for another two years.

Mom lived with his family in Youngstown. Times were hard and there wasn't much money. The stark contrast between beautiful Germany and a drab, steel-producing industrial town must have been quite a shock, visually as well as culturally. Mom didn't speak English and was trying to fit in with an African-American family. Once again my heart went out to her. At the same time, my pride and respect for her accomplishments rose.

Mom learned how to speak English by watching car-toons. Many people think she's from England because her accent is so slight. She was in a new country with a brand new son, and before long, with a mentally retarded daughter. The vague racism of Germany was replaced by the full force of discrimination in America.

Briefly my memory found me sitting in a kindergarten class with my Mom standing in the doorway. She was so beautiful. A little girl leaned over and whispered in my ear, "I didn't know your mother was white!"

I clearly remember thinking, "I didn't know she was white either!"

Color was never an issue in our home. Until it was pointed out to me, I never noticed the difference in color between my mother and father. And racial differences didn't cause their marriage to sour. Like so many other married couples, poor communication and insensitivities on both parts lead to their estrangement.

At last I drifted off to sleep, understanding better than ever what my mother had experienced as a young woman.

A Trip In Time

"Mom," I said the next morning, "I want to see the orphanage."

"Well, that's a shock!" Mom looked surprised. "I tried to get your brother and sister to go with me when they were here but they weren't interested."

It had been fifty-five years since she had seen the orphanage. I could sense both dread and excitement within her as we pulled into the quaint community. We rounded a corner and an enormous yellow building with white windows appeared before us. She didn't have to point it out. It seemed oversized and out of place.

Mom was the first one out of the car. She looked like a time-traveler, hearing voices and picturing faces of long ago that we could not see. Here and there were Catholic nuns dressed in their black and white habits. Mom shuddered and said, "There go those mean old nuns!"

Walking towards the back of the facility, Mom grabbed my arm and pointed to a large stone altar with a statue of the Virgin Mary housed inside. "Look," she exclaimed, "that's where we came every morning for our devotions, no matter what the weather was like. I can't believe that it looks the same." We stood silently inside the grotto as she touched familiar places.

"Mom," I said, "there's a nun coming out of the back door. Let's see if we can go inside." Mom explained to the nun that she had once lived in the orphanage and asked for permission to enter, which was quickly granted.

The halls were wide, dull, and cold. We stopped at the door of the kitchen. "I spent many mornings in here helping to prepare the food," Mom remembered.

The entrance way had a winding staircase with a wrought iron balcony. Mom opened the door across from the bottom of the stairs and said, "Before the bombs started dropping, the air-raid sirens would go off. All of us children would have to rush down these winding stairs and into this room so we could find our shoes and coats in the pitch dark. Then we would go to the basement and wait until the bombing stopped."

I climbed halfway up the winding stairs and called, "Come on, Mom, let's take a picture."

After the photo was snapped, Mom said, "It's ironic that out of all my children, you would be the one who returned with me to the orphanage."

After touring the entire property and heading for the car, Mom paused beside a high wall, "This is the wall I told you about. It looks big now but you can imagine what it seemed like to a little child. For me, it always blocked the sun. Everyday I dreamed of leaving here, and about the wonderful life I would have when I was no longer confined to this dungeon."

Tears flooded my eyes. I pictured the little girl trying to see over the never-ending wall. She did leave one day, but her life had not been so wonderful. And I had been a part of that broken dream. I wished for a moment that I could do it all over again.

Coming Home

Eight days quickly passed, days filled with wonderful sightseeing and meetings with warm and happy people. But the personal victory of having spent a peaceful week alone with Mom caused me to rejoice most of all. Standing in the hallway of Mina's house, it was time for our goodbyes. Mom asked for everyone present to hold hands. She said, "Bunny, would you pray for us?" Her request was totally unexpected.

Bowing our heads in prayer, I thanked God for our tremendous time together and asked for traveling grace. Silently, however, I stood in awe of the God that I serve; the God who can do anything but fail.

Shortly after returning home, a card from Mom arrived. It pictured two champagne glasses being clicked together in a toast. Between the glasses Mom had written, "This is lemonade (smile)."

Inside the card the words read, "I love you and that's something to celebrate!"

Closing the card and tucking it neatly in the envelope, an emotional flood of thanksgiving began to wash over my soul. "Dear Lord", I whispered, "your Word is true and faithful. You promised that 'Love never fails'. I know now that you meant unconditional love. By dying to myself and loving Mom without any thought of return, You have allowed me to witness the power of that love and watch You penetrate into her heart and mind. I'm free Lord. For the first time in my life I am free! The bitterness and anger that would cause my stomach to tie up in knots with just the mention of her name, is gone. Love, God's love, has set me free to be all that You intended me to be. Everything I have been through; the rejection, fear, doubts, and anxiety were all worth it to reach this point. Your ways really are past finding out. To have physically died and never have experienced this victory would have been a great loss for me and Your kingdom. Whatever the future may hold, Lord, I already know the key. It's unconditional love."

At the time, my own release from Bitterness seemed paramount in my mind. But I was soon to discover that my experience would deeply benefit others, too. For the first time in my life, I could face their questions about betrayal without fear. And with time, I was able to share some of the answers God had given me.

Chapter Ten

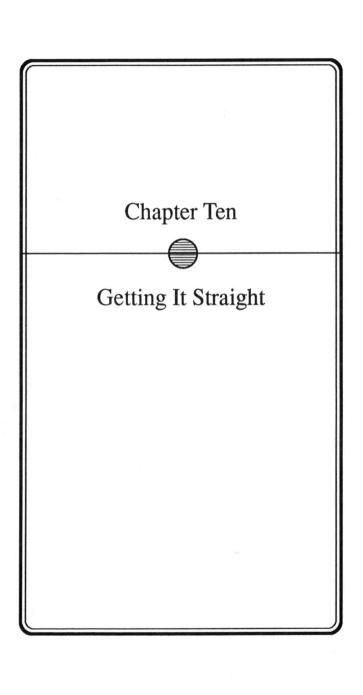

Getting It Straight

Chapter Ten

GETTING IT STRAIGHT

Q. *In your book, you refer to the "commitments of protection" we make when we are betrayed. You say these commitments are designed to protect us from being hurt in the same way again. Also, these commitments "freeze our emotions and effect every relationship from that time forward." I was molested as a child and made a commitment to never allow my children to be placed in a vulnerable situation where the same thing might happen to them. Was there anything wrong with making that commitment?*

A. Absolutely not. There is a difference between a "commitment of protection" and a "commitment to wisdom". In your situation, a "commitment of protection" that would have negatively affected your life would have sounded like this: I'll never allow a man to touch me again! Obviously, that would keep you from enjoying a normal healthy relationship with any person of the opposite sex including your future husband. One true story highlights the dangers of "commitments of protection".

Ruth was an incest victim. When she had her daughter Laney, she made a commitment that she would kill any man who tried to sexually molest Laney. As her daughter grew older, Ruth was honest with Laney about what had happened to her when she was a child. She taught Laney how to protect herself and let her know that if anyone ever attempted to molest her that she would personally kill him. There were two people in the world that Laney loved deeply, her mother and grandfather. As Laney began to bloom into her teens, her grandfather molested her. Knowing her mother's commitment to kill any man who would do such a thing, Laney refused to tell her mother. Laney continued to be molested until she was old enough to leave her mother's house. Because Ruth was controlled by bitterness and not forgiveness, she inadvertently imprisoned her daughter in her hatred. The results were the same.

A "commitment to wisdom" lets us look at our situation through the eyes of forgiveness and unconditional love. In doing so, we structure sound guidelines for ourselves and those we love.

Q. *You say in your book that after loving your mother unconditionally for one year, your daughter wanted to spend a week with her. You told your daughter that you would go with her to spend the day but that she couldn't spend time alone with her grandmother. Why was that?*

A. As in the previous answer, that was a "commitment to wisdom" not a "commitment of protection." Although I had forgiven my mother and was committed to loving her unconditionally, I knew that she was still bitter. My hope, of course, was that in time it would pass. Until it did, however, I felt it important to protect my children from statements that would undermine my authority as their mother, challenging my ability to effectively raise them. I did not mind their spending time with their grandmother, but it was important that the time was limited and monitored.

Q. *I haven't been to church in years because of a bad experience. After spending a great deal of time serving my former church, I felt betrayed when I discovered the leadership was less than reputable. I have been very bitter and even refused to attend weddings and funerals. When I see anyone that represents the clergy, I become livid. There was a time when I was in fellowship with Christ, and I realize now that I gave that up when I decided to want vindication more than fellowship with Christ. I want a fresh start but the road to recovery seems never ending. How do I start taking the first steps?*

A. You can first begin by acquiring a healthy outlook on the purpose of clergy and the church. My pastor says, "The church is a hospital full of sin-sick souls. Some are getting better because they take their medicine (reading and practicing the Word of God). Some are not any better than on the day they walked in because they live according to the flesh not the Spirit."

We attend the local church in obedience to Hebrews 10:25 which says, "Forsake not the assembling of yourselves together." It also tells us in Acts 2:47 that the Lord added to the church as many as were saved.

There will always be unscrupulous people in the church. It especially hurts when it reaches the level of the clergy. However, if we never lose sight of our purpose for attending, it will do three things.

> 1. Keep us focused. Our purpose is to worship, praise, learn and serve. "And whatever you do, do it all to the glory of God". If our service is done so that we will be recognized and appreciated by man, we will inevitably be disappointed. But if the service we perform is to please God, no matter what man does, we have a

sense of satisfaction in knowing we were acting in obedience to Him.

2. Direct our focus in worship. If we are not careful, it is easy for us to make the leadership "mini gods." Although they are intended to be messengers of God, they are not God. If we lose sight of that, when they fall short it can cause our whole world to crumble. I'm pretty sure when you look back in retrospect, there were some obvious signs that you overlooked. We miss certain warnings when we are out of focus.

3. Pray for direction. When we know the purpose for attending church, it should cause us to be circumspect in who we choose as our leadership. It is all right to ask questions regarding the integrity of the church's leadership.

Q. *My uncle sexually molested me when I was growing up. I want to be free of the bitterness I have felt over the years. After reading your book, I know that I must go and talk with him. Suppose he denies that it ever happened, what should I do?*

A. You have asked a very difficult question. The steps of correcting this situation will not be easy. Make sure that you go in a spirit of reconciliation, not judgment. In this situation, it is always safer to take someone with you. Let him know honestly how his actions have affected your life. If he is repentant, find out if he has sought counselling for his problem. Let him know that if he has not received counselling, it would have to take place in order for you not to expose his deeds. If, however, he denies the action or refuses to get counselling, it will be necessary for you to contact your family members, especially those who have children.

A friend of mine has lovely parents. I cared for and respected them deeply. I had known them for eight years when I became aware that my friend had been sexually molested by her father. Although I felt compassion for her situation, it greatly concerned me that she had never made me aware of her situation. I have four daughters and on two occasions I had allowed her parents to babysit them. Because of her fear of exposing her father she put my children in harm's way.

I know it will probably take every ounce of courage to do what is necessary. You may possibly have to endure ridicule from family members who may discount your claim. But if you save another child from experiencing the trauma of being molested, it will have been worth it. If more people were exposed for this hideous deed, we could possibly begin to turn the tide on a situation which is rapidly approaching epidemic proportions.

Q. *When our mother passed away, all of my brothers and sisters began to squabble over her assets. It caused a great division that still exists today. I haven't spoken to my sisters in four years. Since that time, I have become a Christian. I felt they betrayed me and everything that my mother stood for. I have been pleased with my spiritual development, that was until I read your book and realized that I was sacrificing fellowship with Christ by allowing this unforgiveness to remain in my heart. My question is, where do I begin to fix this mess?*

A. I always suggest that the first step is prayer. There is no pat answer because each situation is different. When God knows that you want to obey Him by bringing reconciliation to this situation, He will guide you in the specific steps you should take. There are, however, some usual steps that should be taken.

1. Give up your right to judge why your brothers and sisters did what they did. Forgive them in your heart.

2. Confess your fault in harboring resentment and hurt.

3. When you contact them, make sure that your only goal is reconciliation.

4. Be committed to loving them unconditionally. You won't be as likely to be hurt if you are not expecting anything in return, and that includes a kind word.

5. When you are not looking for a particular response, you can't be disappointed and it will allow the Holy Spirit time to bring about reconciliation in the relationship.

6. Always have a spirit of gratitude as you observe the slightest bit of thawing in the relationships and remember, we all see through "a dark mirror," and things may be better than you think.

7. Remember that the reason you've been hurt so deeply is because of the depth of your love for them. Don't let another day

pass without taking the steps to contact
one of them.

Q. *I have so many clocks from my first marriage that I
don't know where to put them all. I married the woman
of my dreams and never thought I would be a divorcee. I
worked hard to provide for her and the children. Imagine
my shock when I discovered she was having an affair with
one of my co-workers. I was willing to forgive her and go
on with our lives, but she wanted a divorce. I felt so
betrayed! When the divorce was final, I had so many
"commitments of protection" that another relationship or
marriage was out of the question. That is until I met this
wonderful woman. I would love to spend the rest of my
life with her but it would be unfair to bring my mantel full
of "clocks" into the relationship. My wife has remarried
and her husband is a very jealous man. Getting in touch
with her to have a conversation about anything but the
children is out of the question. How do I get free?*

A. In a situation like this, or if it involves someone
betrayed by a person who is now deceased, your release
is mental. If your first wife's husband would misinterpret
your intentions in "getting it straight" with your ex-wife,
then wisdom would dictate that you take another route.
Scripture encourages us to "esteem one another higher
than ourselves."

First, confess to yourself your attitude when you felt
betrayed. Were you angry, mean-spirited, bitter, harsh?
Ask God to forgive you and be willing to move on. After
you decide to give up your right to judge why she did what
she did, then purpose in your mind to love her unconditionally with no thought of anything in return. Replace all
negative and bitter thoughts with those of kindness,
gentleness, and love. I am sure your children will notice
the marked difference in your attitude and spirit and in

their own ways communicate with your ex-wife that you are no longer angry or bitter. If an opportunity arises for you to do a kind deed, then by all means, do so with no thought of anything in return.

Forgiveness will tear down the wall of distrust towards the opposite sex. Make sure to love your new wife unconditionally and ask the Lord to show you where you may have fallen short in your first marriage so that you can correct it. Instead of worrying that you may be betrayed again, have forgiveness and unconditional love ready, in case that circumstance should arise.

Q. *It's hard to believe that I can be a teenager and relate to your book so well. The kids at school wonder why I prefer to hang out with the guys more than the girls. Well, now I know that I have a clock sitting on the fireplace of my heart and it is set to January 12th, 1989.*

That is when my best girlfriend shared one of my most intimate secrets with another girl, to get to me again. While I was at a weekend Christian camp recently, someone gave me your book. As I read it, I knew that my "commitment of protection" would affect my whole life. I want to get rid of my clock but loathe the thought of having to speak to this girl. I haven't said a word to her since it happened. I know I don't want to spend my Christian life "socializing" with Jesus. Is there an easier way out of this than talking to her?

A. Unfortunately, no. Many of us have wounds from being verbally stabbed by a friend we trusted in. Most of our readers can relate to your pain; however, a determination to right a wrong relationship is one of the strongest signs that Christ has made a difference in your life. Your situation is probably one of the more common occurrences in relationships and it destroys many friendships. This is mostly due to our not handling the situation according to God's Word. Don't forget Matthew 5:23,24 says, "Therefore if thou bring thy gift to the altar and there remember that thy brother has ought against thee, leave there thy gift before the altar and go thy way; first be reconciled to thy brother and then come and offer thy gift."

We should talk only with the one who hurt us although it is really tempting to hear someone else take our side. When you meet, let her know how deeply you were hurt. Remember there is nothing in wrong with confrontation while telling the person that you forgive them for it.

Ask her to forgive you for the feelings of anger and bitterness towards her. Remember, you are not going for a response but for reconciliation.

One of the worst possible scenarios is that she laughs at you and then tells someone that you came begging for her friendship back. As terrible as that might sound it doesn't come close to the humiliation Christ suffered as He hung on the cross.

Once you have acknowledged your hurt and asked for forgiveness, your part is done. You are free to go. The next step, however, is unconditional love. That doesn't mean that she's supposed to be your best friend again, although there's no reason why she can't be your friend. Just be careful in the future of the quality of your relationship before you reveal intimate information.

I have a wonderful friend who has great difficulty in keeping information to herself. I love her for her strengths but make it a point not to tell her anything I wouldn't want repeated. I hope that as she grows in Christ that area of her life will be strengthened. Until it is, however, I do my best not to feed her weakness, nevertheless she's a great friend and I appreciate her for what she brings to the relationship.

Q. *What if you are not the betrayed but the betrayor? Several years ago, I committed adultery. I have a wonderful wife but an attractive woman crossed my path and one thing led to another. My wife says that she has forgiven me but I am plagued with guilt. How do I accept the forgiveness she has so graciously extended to me?*

A. Your feeling of guilt is understandable. Proverbs 6:31-32 says,

> "But whoso committeth adultery with a woman (or man) lacketh understanding; he that doeth it destroyeth his own soul. A wound and dishonor shall he get; and his reproach shall not be wiped away."

As bleak as that may sound, it should only heighten our appreciation for God's grace that covers a multitude of sins and for His nature that He shares with each of His children. Forgiveness is a holy act and when we exercise it in our lives, it is a taste of the Divine. Your wife has chosen to apply forgiveness to your sin against her and God. She is a special woman.

If you choose to reciprocate with guilt, it will cause you to hide your emotions and your shame will make you withdraw. By using God's Word as our guideline, we find that forgiveness should endear us to the person, not push us away. When Mary, who had been a wicked woman opened a bottle of expensive perfume and anointed the feet of Jesus, His disciples complained that the money could be used for better purposes.

Jesus' response was, "this woman loves me much because I have forgiven her much." His forgiveness had caused Mary to respond with great appreciation, not with hiding in shame of what she had done.

As the years go by and people admire the love between you and your wife, you may sometimes be asked, "How did you come to love your wife so deeply?" Without hesitation, you should be able to gladly proclaim, "I love her much because she has forgiven me much." Accept the precious gift of forgiveness that comes from God and do as Jesus commanded. "Go and sin no more."

Chapter Eleven

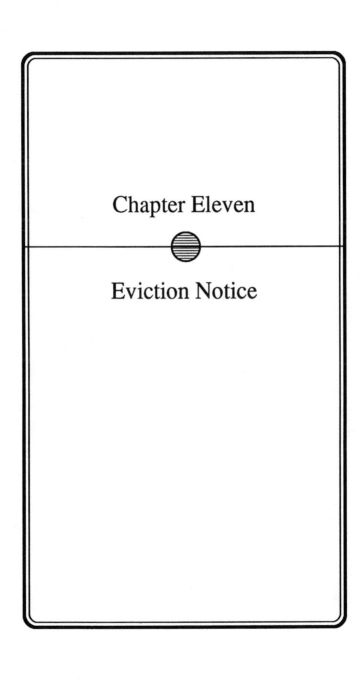

Eviction Notice

Chapter Eleven

EVICTION NOTICE

For these past chapters, you have walked with me through some very disturbing days, months, and years of my life. This book was not intended to provide you with unpracticed scriptural teachings on forgiveness and unconditional love. Its purpose was to take you, by example, through a process so you could realistically see the suffering, pain and victory that comes when you want to know Christ intimately in the "power of His resurrection" and in the "fellowship of His sufferings". You have to want to know Him more than you want to reserve your right to be angry, bitter, vindictive, or reclusive.

Perhaps Bitterness has been living rent-free in your life. I pray that you make a decision to be rid of its destructive presence. In my mind's eye, I can see you marching towards your camouflaged door. Bitterness hears your firm footsteps and decides to take a peek down the hall.

In a loud whisper it hisses, "Hey, Anger, Revenge, Hate, get over here!"

Bitterness sees that you're headed its way. There's something about your face that alarms it. And what's that you're carrying in your hand?

With a mighty shove, you throw the door open, causing Bitterness and its friends to fly across the room, taking out your spiritual hammer, you tack a paper to the wall that reads "EVICTION NOTICE!"

As Bitterness eases forward to read the edict, its trembling causes Anger to shout, "Oh, don't get so excited! Haven't you seen that book on forgiveness and unconditional love, lying around? Nothing's going to happen to us, these things always pass and..."

Bitterness cuts Anger off. It raises its long scaly finger and points to the signature and says, "But look who signed this thing."

As their eyes travel to the bottom of the page, they screech in unison, "In Jesus' Name!"

Yes, in Jesus' name. When you make the decision to forgive and unconditionally love the person who has betrayed you, you can post an eviction notice in the room where Bitterness lives. It will have to leave or starve to death. Bitterness feeds on anger, revenge, and hate.

When most people are honest, they have to admit that they have been so badly hurt by their betrayals because they have loved so deeply. Usually it's a father, mother, sister, brother, husband, wife, boyfriend, girlfriend, or child who has betrayed us. These are all people who have been close to us and have been given the opportunity to touch our emotions.

This raises an inevitable question: "Why should I have to be the one to do the forgiving and the unconditional loving? Haven't I suffered enough already?"

I can think of no better reason than this; we all should want to follow in Jesus' footsteps. He made His point abundantly clear when the self-righteous Jewish teachers of His day questioned Him. As recorded in Mark 12:28, one of them hoped to trip Him up with a profound question:

> One of the teachers of the law came and
> heard them debating. Noticing that Jesus
> had given them a good answer, he asked

Him, Of all the commandments, which is
the most important?

That really is a very interesting question. Among those
present, I wonder how many of the others would have
given His answer.

"The most important commandment," answered Jesus,
"is this:

> "Hear, O Israel, the Lord your God, the
> Lord is one. Love the Lord your God with
> all your heart and with all your soul and
> with all your strength. The second is this:
> Love your neighbor as yourself. There is
> no commandment greater than these."

When we love the Lord with all our heart, soul, mind,
and strength, what remaining portion of us can be unfor-
giving and unloving?

Many times our need to respond in love to a situation
is silenced by a mantel full of clocks placed there in the
midst of past betrayals. Our bitterness forbids us to get
close enough to even pick one of them up. We are for-
tified by our "commitments of protection" so that we are
never placed in the same vulnerable position of being hurt
again.

Making The Right Choice

Usually the first steps in ridding ourselves of Bitterness are the most difficult. We have to push open the
camouflaged door and be willing to look at the betrayal
that lies hidden inside. Once we have identified the per-
petrator(s), we need to realize that if we decide to hold on
to Bitterness, we are relinquishing precious fellowship
with Christ.

What grudge in your life is of more value than sweet fellowship with Jesus? Think about it.

Christ died for our sins, gave us eternal life. He stands at the door of our hearts, knocking continuously so that He can commune with us. Jesus is everything He promised to be.

He is our love (John 15:9).

He is our peace (John 14:27).

He is our joy (John 15:11).

Yet we can never know Him in His fullness if Bitterness lives anywhere within us.

Once you have taken a look at your betrayal and have decided that you want Christ more than your right to be bitter, you will need to take some steps. After identifying those who have hurt you:

1. Arrange a time to meet with them. Do not write a letter. Letters can be stored and read over and over, many times keeping wounds open. The purpose of the meeting is to allow the spirit of reconciliation to begin the process of healing the relationship. Go in that spirit. If they live at a distance, a telephone call may need to take the place of a personal visit.

2. Acknowledge any faults you may have had in the breakdown of the relationship. For example, you might want to admit that you've been holding anger and bitterness towards them for what was done to you. You should also acknowledge any wrongdoing on your part.

3. Ask them to forgive you. How they respond is not important. They probably have not made the decision you've made and therefore may not want to express forgiveness.

4. Allow the other person to share honestly without being defensive. In a word; LISTEN. They may claim no wrongdoing on their part. But remember Proverbs 16:2: "Every man's ways are right in his own sight." It is the job of the Holy Spirit to convict people of sin.

5. Go with the understanding that no matter how the meeting ends, you are committed to loving that person unconditionally. Remember Luke 6:35: "Love your enemies, do good and lend, expecting nothing in return. Then your reward will be great, and you will be sons of the Most High for even your Father in heaven is merciful to the unkind and the ungrateful. Therefore, be ye merciful even as He is merciful."

6. If the person who betrayed you is deceased, your process will be mental but nonetheless effective. Do not be afraid to remember how you were hurt. Place it at the foot of God's altar and make the decision to forgive.

From that moment on, whenever you think of that person, replace negative

thoughts with ones of love and kindness.
Love them unconditionally in your mind.
You may be surprised what doors of explanation the Lord opens to you so that
you will have a greater understanding and
compassion for that person.

I Have Already Forgiven

Often a sincere Christian will approach me and say
something like, "How many times am I going to have to
forgive this person? I think it's settled and then when I
see them or hear something they've said, I have a complete relapse. It seems like I'm right back to square one!
How can I know I have really forgiven someone?"

When I ask them to retrace their steps of forgiveness,
it usually ends with them simply turning that person over
to the Lord and announcing they are taking their hands off
the whole thing. I ask, "After you forgave them, did you
begin to love them, expecting nothing in return?"

The answer has usually been, "No".

Forgiving with expected results sets us up for disappointment. We must be willing to accept the fact that in
our lifetime we may never see change occur. Some people
have not repented of their wrongdoing until they've
remorsefully looked down into the casket of a loved one
they have betrayed.

If I had been looking for any confirmation of change
in my mother, one particular phone conversation with her
would have shattered me.

Over three years had passed since I began loving Mom
unconditionally. I was invited to be the Woman's Day
speaker at a church in New York, and the girls were ac-
companying me on the trip. On the way to the airport, we
stopped at Mom's house to give her some Mother's Day

gifts since we would be out of town that Sunday. It was a pleasant visit.

Upon my return from New York, I called Mom. She was noticeably upset soon into our conversation. Finally she snapped, "What's wrong with Fawn, anyway? Does she need to see a psychiatrist?"

Stunned by the sharp question, I asked, "What do you mean Mom?"

She replied, "Did you see the Mother's Day card Fawn gave me? Her handwriting is so small." I wondered if Mom had been reading articles on graphology.

"I saw the card Mom," I answered, "but I didn't see what she wrote in it."

"I'll be right back," she said and put the telephone down. Upon her return, she read, "Dear Grandma, Thank you for all you have done for my mother. You did a good job. Love, Fawn."

Pausing for a few seconds, I tried to figure out why Mom was so disturbed by Fawn's sentiments. My daughter's words were very special to me. It had only been a short time since she had run away, and I had unconditionally loved her through her difficulties. Now we were on great terms and our relationship was moving forward in a positive way.

Then I remembered Bitterness.

When the object of our bitterness receives praise, it causes us to feel anger and hostility. Deep inside, we always want the person who betrayed us to pay for what he or she has done. Fawn was openly praising me, and it had been a long time since I had seen my mother so upset.

Over the past three years, there had been no intense conversation between us. My only goal had been to love Mom. I never brought up the past. Now Mom began to rehearse some of the things she had said to me the

memorable night of our first encounter. As she continual-
ly pressed on my scars, I rejoiced that the pain was gone.
The only agony I felt lay in my awareness that she was
still in bondage to Bitterness.

"When you were thirteen years old, you told me you
hated me and wished I never was your mother!" shouted
Mom. "You don't know how bad that hurt."

I silently whispered a prayer and responded with a statement she had made three years prior. It was the first time
I had ever mentioned it. "Mom, do you remember when
you said to me, 'If I had to do it all over again, I never
would have had you?' Those words hurt so bad that I went
home and cried for three days."

Mom quickly reacted. "That couldn't possibly have
hurt you as much as you hurt me!"

Had I not made the decision to love Mom unconditionally, I would have lost control. I would have shouted,
"Really? And just where did you buy your measuring
stick? Who says you were hurt more? My statement was
made to you when I was thirteen years old. Your statement was made to me when you were sixty years old! Now
who do you think meant it more?"

Fotrunately, by God's grace, those words were never
said. Instead I replied, "No, Mom, it really hurt. I came
home and cried for three days."

At this point something astounding happened. Mom
said, "I have to go now and fix dinner for Eddie."

I answered, "I know you have to go, Mom, but before
you do, I want you to see what has just taken place. I said,
'I went home and cried for three days,' and you said, 'I
have to go and fix dinner for Eddie.' You asked me why
I had so many emotional outbursts as a child. It was because when I came to you hurt or in need, you would either
change the subject or walk out of the room."

Mom answered, "Eddie gets really upset when the dinner is not ready on time."

Incredibly, I realized that Mom was in a full-blown state of denial. She actually could not see how she had hurt and wounded me over the years. From her vantage point, everything done to her was unprovoked and undeserved.

"Mom, I'm going to let you go. But before I do, I want you to know that there is nothing you can say or do that will change my love for you."

As I hung up the telephone, miraculously there was no anger or pain.

I rejoiced that being free of Bitterness was allowing me to deal with some very sensitive issues. The next morning Mom called at an unusual time—6:30 a.m. She telephoned just to say hello, without mentioning the conversation from the day before.

I knew the Lord was penetrating into her heart, just as He often did into mine. The journey is not over yet, not for either one of us. But I think we're both committed to the end.

Passing Judgment

There is another aspect of *unforgiveness* that should encourage us to release every person who might ever have betrayed us. Matthew 7:12 says:

> "Judge ye not, lest ye be judged. For with the same measure you judge, it will be measured back to you."

In order to have unforgiveness in our hearts, we will first have to pass judgment upon the person who hurt us. We always try to take into consideration all the reasons they may have had to betray us. Many times we will spend hours trying to figure out what motivated their actions against us. The process is painful and usually results in feelings of anger and frustration. We judge those who hurt us and hold them in bondage in our hearts.

When we judge the actions of another person, a scriptural principle goes into effect. We too will be judged, perhaps not by the same person we judged. But somehow, somewhere, someone will sit in judgment of us.

When we choose to forgive people who have betrayed us, we actually give up our right to judge them. And to do so is to experience one of the most liberating feelings imaginable.

Matthew 6:14-15 says,

> "For if you forgive men when they sin against you, your heavenly Father will also forgive you. But if you do not forgive men their sins, your Father will also forgive your sins."

Forgiveness and unconditional love are given to us freely by the Father. It is only natural that He would want us to pass it on. Considering all the things we have done wrong against Him, what can be our justification for not forgiving others?"

Going Home

With regards to the removal of Bitterness, one last word of encouragement can be found in II Peter 3:8:

> "One day in heaven is like a thousand years on earth."

When we acknowledged that we were sinners (Romans 3:23) and confessed with our mouths that Jesus was Lord and was risen from the dead (Romans 10:9), we were given eternal life. Our citizenship changed from earth to heaven, and we became pilgrims traveling through a barren land.

II Peter 3:8 says that when one day passes in heaven, it is like a thousand years passing on earth. That means that if you lived to be seventy years old here, only one hour and forty-eight minutes would have passed in heaven! No wonder Paul said in Romans 8:18-19,

> "I consider that our present sufferings are not worthy to be compared with the glory that will be revealed in us."

Many of us have less than an hour left to be obedient to what God has called us to do — to forgive and love unconditionally. Many of us are running a little short on hope. Sharing the suffering of Jesus can be painful, and sometimes we grow "weary in well-doing". Maybe we need a spiritual vacation!

I consider myself a travel agent. My travel brochure is neatly tucked away at the back of every Bible in Revelation 21:10-22:5. My desire is to get as many people as I can to go home to heaven with me and also to take time to contemplate what a wonderful future we have in store for us.

In those Scriptures, the Apostle John is caught up in the Spirit and allowed to see heaven. He saw an angel measure the walls, and they were 1,500 miles high, wide and deep. The wall of the city is jasper, a clear stone, which means you can see into the city. That wall is held up by twelve foundations, each a precious stone such as a sapphire, emerald, ruby and topaz.

I once asked my husband, Frank, "Do you think it's talking about a bunch of tiny stones?"

He answered, "No, I think it's like the rainbow where one color runs into the other."

There are three gates on each side — on the east, west, north and south. Each gate is one solid sheet of pearl with an angel standing beside it. Don't you wonder which gate you will go in ... and what the angel will say to you?

The city and the streets are pure gold like clear glass. We have never seen that kind of gold. Even our most expensive gold has impurities in it.

There is a river that springs from underneath the throne of God and flows down the middle of the city, clear as crystal. Have you ever seen the sun reflect off of a piece of crystal? The colors dance against the walls.

Yet in heaven, there is no sun by day, no moon by night. Heaven is lit by the glory of God which is a thousand times brighter than the sun. God's glory shines through a city of pure gold, reflecting off of a flowing river that is clear as crystal!

In the middle of the street, and on each side of the river there is the tree of life with twelve fruits growing on it at the same time. Exquisite seraphim and cherubim angels are all around and there is no hunger, thirst or tiredness. There will be no dying there, and God will dry all of our tears.

Jesus promised in John 14:1:

> "Let not your heart be troubled. Trust in God; trust also in Me. In My Father's house are many mansions; if it were not so, I would have told you. I go to prepare a place for you that where I am, there you may be also."

The Final Chapter

My friend, I believe that as you've read through this book, the Holy Spirit has shown you who you need to forgive and love unconditionally. I already know that doing so won't be easy for you, but removing Bitterness is absolutely imperative if you are going to know Christ in the "power of His resurrection and the fellowship of His suffering."

Page 26 will remain blank until you have made your personal decision to live in forgiveness and unconditional love. That page is for your story.

Once you have taken the steps to destroy Bitterness in your life, you will return strong enough to write your own account.

Then and only then will this book be complete.